THE CIVIL RIGHTS MOVEMENT

Other books in the
Opposing Viewpoints in World History series:

OPPOSING VIEWPOINTS®
IN WORLD HISTORY

THE CIVIL RIGHTS MOVEMENT

Jill Karson, *Book Editor*

Bruce Glassman, *Vice President*
Bonnie Szumski, *Publisher*
Helen Cothran, *Managing Editor*

OPPOSING
VIEWPOINTS®
SERIES

GREENHAVEN PRESS
An imprint of Thomson Gale, a part of The Thomson Corporation

THOMSON
—— ✳ ——™
GALE

Detroit • New York • San Francisco • San Diego • New Haven, Conn.
Waterville, Maine • London • Munich

35 93040

LIBRARY OF CONGRESS CATALOGING-IN-PUBLICATION DATA

The civil rights movement / Jill Karson, book editor.
    p. cm. — (Opposing viewpoints in world history)
Includes bibliographical references and index.
ISBN 0-7377-2578-8 (pbk. : alk. paper) — ISBN 0-7377-2577-X (lib. : alk. paper)
    1. African Americans—Civil rights—History—Twentieth century. 2. Civil rights movements—United States—History—Twentieth century. 3. United States—Race relations. 4. African Americans—Civil rights—History—Twentieth century—Sources. 5. Civil rights movements—United States—History—Twentieth century—Sources. 6. United States—Race relations—Sources. I. Karson, Jill. II. Opposing viewpoints in world history series.
E185.61.C6145 2005
323.1196'073—dc22   2004049715

Printed in the United States of America

✸ Contents

schools and undermined the long-term effort to remedy discrimination in American society.

Chapter 3: What Were the Strategies of the Civil Rights Movement?

Foreword

On December 2, 1859, several hundred soldiers gathered at the outskirts of Charles Town, Virginia, to carry out, and provide security for, the execution of a shabbily dressed old man with a beard that hung to his chest. The execution of John Brown quickly became and has remained one of those pivotal historical events that are immersed in controversy. Some of Brown's contemporaries claimed that he was a religious fanatic who deserved to be executed for murder. Others claimed Brown was a heroic and selfless martyr whose execution was a tragedy. Historians have continued to debate which picture of Brown is closest to the truth.

The wildly diverging opinions on Brown arise from fundamental disputes involving slavery and race. In 1859 the United States was becoming increasingly polarized over the issue of slavery. Brown believed in both the necessity of violence to end slavery and in the full political and social equality of the races. This made him part of the radical fringe even in the North. Brown's conviction and execution stemmed from his role in leading twenty-one white and black followers to attack and occupy a federal weapons arsenal in Harpers Ferry, Virginia. Brown had hoped to ignite a large slave uprising. However, the raid begun on October 16, 1859, failed to draw support from local slaves; after less than thirty-six hours, Brown's forces were overrun by federal and local troops. Brown was wounded and captured, and ten of his followers were killed.

Brown's raid—and its intent to arm slaves and foment insurrection—was shocking to the South and much of the North. An editorial in the *Patriot*, an Albany, Georgia, newspaper, stated that Brown was a "notorious old thief and murderer" who deserved to be hanged. Many southerners expressed fears that Brown's actions were part of a broader northern conspiracy against the South—fears that seemed to be confirmed by captured letters documenting Brown's ties with some prominent northern abolitionists, some of whom had provided him with financial support. Such alarms also found confirmation in the pronouncements of some speakers such as writer Henry David Thoreau, who asserted that

Brown had "a perfect right to interfere by force with the slave-holder, in order to rescue the slave." But not all in the North defended Brown's actions. Abraham Lincoln and William Seward, leading politicians of the nascent Republican Party, both denounced Brown's raid. Abolitionists, including William Lloyd Garrison, called Brown's adventure "misguided, wild, and apparently insane." They were afraid Brown had done serious damage to the abolitionist cause.

Today, though all agree that Brown's ideas on racial equality are no longer radical, historical opinion remains divided on just what Brown thought he could accomplish with his raid, or even whether he was fully sane. Historian Russell Banks argues that even today opinions of Brown tend to split along racial lines. African Americans tend to view him as a hero, Banks argues, while whites are more likely to judge him mad. "And it's for the same reason—because he was a white man who was willing to sacrifice his life to liberate Black Americans. The very thing that makes him seem mad to white Americans is what makes him seem heroic to Black Americans."

The controversy over John Brown's life and death remind readers that history is replete with debate and controversy. Not only have major historical developments frequently been marked by fierce debates as they happened, but historians examining the same events in retrospect have often come to opposite conclusions about their causes, effects, and significance. By featuring both contemporaneous and retrospective disputes over historical events in a pro/con format, the Opposing Viewpoints in World History series can help readers gain a deeper understanding of important historical issues, see how historical judgments unfold, and develop critical thinking skills. Each article is preceded by a concise summary of its main ideas and information about the author. An in-depth book introduction and prefaces to each chapter provide background and context. An annotated table of contents and index help readers quickly locate material of interest. Each book also features an extensive bibliography for further research, questions designed to spark discussion and promote close reading and critical thinking, and a chronology of events.

✵ Introduction

The civil rights movement that spanned the years following the *Brown v. Board of Education* decision of 1954 through the passage of the Voting Rights Act of 1965 marked a watershed period that accomplished far more than the elimination of racial barriers; it led to the overwhelming transformation of American social, cultural, and political life. Changes to prevailing notions about the citizenship rights of blacks, for example, coupled with a redefinition of the role of the government and courts in protecting these rights, continue to bolster the human rights of all Americans, regardless of their skin color.

The words *civil rights* often conjure images of Martin Luther King Jr. delivering his soul-stirring "I Have a Dream" speech before the nation's capital. On a darker note, many recall television footage of peaceful marchers beset by fire hoses and snarling police dogs, or the resolute faces of black college students as they waged their sit-in campaigns at southern lunch counters. Certainly one of the most trenchant set of images—and perhaps representing the nadir of the movement—are the photographs of four young black schoolgirls who were killed when a bomb ripped through the Sixteenth Street Baptist Church where they were attending Sunday school. These and other images are a testament to the intense burst of black activism—and the resulting white backlash—that characterized the civil rights movement of the mid–twentieth century.

Yet African Americans have always struggled for their rights. Many consider the civil rights movement to have begun not in the 1950s but when Africans were first brought in chains, centuries earlier, to American shores. In particular, those blacks who fought their enslavement and demanded fundamental citizenship rights laid the foundation for the modern civil rights movement.

The Legacy of Slavery

The first slaves were brought to America in 1619. Not until the Thirteenth Amendment abolished slavery following the Civil War

11

did blacks gain their freedom. Yet the newly freed blacks were largely illiterate and bereft of money or property, and racism and inequality were rampant, especially in the South, where slavery had predominated for so long. To aid black assimilation into white society, federal and state governments implemented many democratic reforms between the years 1865 and 1875, the Reconstruction era. The Fourteenth Amendment, for example, guaranteed blacks federally protected equal rights, and the Fifteenth Amendment granted black men the right to vote.

Despite these and other measures to safeguard the former slaves' newfound rights, the gains of the once-promising Reconstruction era were short-lived. In a climate of extreme southern white hegemony, many employed a variety of means to keep blacks from enjoying any of the benefits of citizenship. Some, for example, sought to keep blacks completely disenfranchised through harassment or intimidation. A number of racist groups, such as the vigilante Ku Klux Klan (KKK), used even more harrowing methods—lynching and other forms of violence, for example—to brutalize and terrify blacks seeking to exercise their rights or advance their standing.

As the constitutional guarantees of the Thirteenth, Fourteenth, and Fifteenth amendments continued to erode, the Supreme Court struck perhaps the most crippling blow to the black struggle for equality: In 1896 the Court ruled in *Plessy v. Ferguson* that blacks and whites could be legally separated as long as the facilities for each were "equal." Facilities for blacks and whites, however, were rarely equal. More importantly, the Supreme Court's "separate but equal" doctrine, by legally backing segregation, gave white society a powerful tool to keep blacks from enjoying even the most rudimentary rights of citizenship. With the Supreme Court now reinforcing the South's segregation practices, the environment of white racism gave birth to Jim Crow—southern customs and laws that kept parks, drinking fountains, streetcars, restaurants, theaters, and other public places rigidly segregated.

In response to Jim Crow, which by 1900 extended into all spheres of public life, several leaders in the black community stepped up to debate political strategies to fight injustice and racial inequality. One of the dominant figures of this early movement for civil rights was the fiery intellectual W.E.B. Du Bois, who exhorted blacks to fight for the rights they deserved. Du Bois's crusade led, in part, to the formation of the National Association for the Advancement of Colored People (NAACP), a civil rights organization that brought together lawyers, educators, and activists to collectively fight for black civil rights. Through lobbying, agitation, and legal action, the NAACP continued a steady campaign to end segregation in housing, education, and other areas of public life.

With the outbreak of World War I, well over a quarter of a million black troops joined the military, but were relegated to segregated units. At the same time, many blacks traveled north to take advantage of the burgeoning defense industries. This massive migration, however, aggravated unemployment and other problems that already plagued the northern urban centers. Racial problems continued unabated. When the United States entered World War II, African Americans were, as before, subjected to rampant discrimination in the defense industries and in military units—despite their willingness to risk their lives in combat. These wartime experiences, coupled with the redistribution of the black populace, resulted in a surge of black protest that brought Jim Crow under national scrutiny.

The Birth of a Movement

During the 1950s, two incidents brought the issue of civil rights squarely into the public spotlight. On May 17, 1954, the NAACP, which had been steadily chipping away at the legal foundations of segregation, won an unprecedented legal victory: The Supreme Court unanimously ruled in *Brown v. Board of Education* that segregation in public schools was unconstitutional. Chief Justice Earl Warren presented the Court's decision, in which he describes why "separate but equal" in education represents a violation of black Americans' rights:

> Segregation of white and colored children in public schools has a detrimental effect upon the colored children. The impact is greater when it has the sanction of the law; for the policy of separating the races is usually interpreted as denoting the inferiority of the Negro group. A sense of inferiority af-

fects the motivation of a child to learn. Segregation, with the sanction of law, therefore, has a tendency to inhibit the educational and mental development of Negro children and deprive them of some of the benefits they would receive in a racially integrated school system.

In nullifying the "separate but equal" doctrine set forth in *Plessy v. Ferguson*, the high court had struck an unequivocal blow to segregation. Yet southern racist practices were deeply entrenched, and many whites remained adamantly opposed to change. The implementation of *Brown*, then, remained painstakingly slow, if not nonexistent. Many school officials refused to comply with the ruling, and the threat of harassment—for the ruling had unleashed fierce resistance—prevented many black students from enrolling in all-white schools. At the same time, schools for black students remained overcrowded, dilapidated, and, in general, grossly inferior to those that their white counterparts enjoyed.

The second incident that captured the public eye unfolded in Montgomery, Alabama, where a seamstress named Rosa Parks created the spark that would provide the momentum for the entire civil rights movement. On December 1, 1955, the NAACP member boarded a public bus and took a seat in the "Negro" section in the back of the bus. Later, Parks refused to relinquish her seat to a white passenger, defying the law by which blacks were required to give up their seats to white passengers when the front section, reserved for whites, was filled. Parks was immediately arrested.

In protest, the black community launched a one-day local boycott of Montgomery's public bus system. As support for Parks burgeoned, the NAACP and other black leaders took advantage of the opportunity to draw attention to their cause. They enlisted the help of a relatively unknown preacher, Martin Luther King Jr., to organize and lead a massive resistance movement that would challenge Montgomery's racist laws. Four days after Parks's arrest, the city-wide Montgomery bus boycott began. It lasted for more than a year. Despite taunting and other forms of harassment from the white community, the boycotters persevered until the federal courts intervened and desegregated the buses on December 21, 1956.

The Montgomery bus boycott was important not only because

it struck down a particularly overt Jim Crow law that affected many southern blacks but because it demonstrated that the black community, through unity and determination, could make their voices heard and effect change. Picketing, boycotting, and other forms of resistance spread rapidly to communities throughout the South. Meanwhile, King emerged as the movement's preeminent leader. His adherence to the nonviolent tactics used by the Indian nationalist Mohandas Gandhi would largely characterize the entire civil rights movement and inspire large-scale participation by whites as well as blacks.

The Pace Quickens

From 1955 to 1960, the efforts of blacks to bring attention to their cause met with some success. In 1957 Congress passed the Civil Rights Act—the first since Reconstruction—to establish a civil rights division in the Justice Department that would enforce voting and other rights. Meanwhile, the NAACP continued to challenge the underpinnings of segregation, and a number of new organizations were formed to take up the banner of civil rights. Among these, the Southern Christian Leadership Conference (SCLC), a Christian-based organization founded in 1957 and led by King, became a major force in organizing the civil rights movement.

Other organizations, too, made headway in publicizing the many civil rights abuses that continued to plague southern blacks. The newly formed Student Nonviolent Coordinating Committee (SNCC) grabbed the media spotlight—and triggered a flood of protests—when it backed four students who launched a sit-in campaign to desegregate southern lunch counters. Not only was the nonviolent sit-in technique used to desegregate other public places, but it gave large numbers of black youths a way to participate in the movement. As legions of young African Americans came forward to take part in boycotts, demonstrations, and rallies, expectations swelled. At the same time, the escalating black protest spurred extensive coverage by the national media, bringing black demands before the public eye as never before.

In 1961 the Congress of Racial Equality (CORE) harnessed this rising tide of student activism and sent a band of young volunteers on what became known as freedom rides. These interracial bus trips were designed to test the implementation of laws that prohibited segregation on buses, interstate terminals, and other facilities along the way. Despite their adherence to nonviolence, freedom riders were met with open hostility. Many were jailed. Far more harrowing, however, was the real threat of violence. One group encountered a mob in Alabama that set the riders' bus on fire, and proceeded to beat them as they fled the burning vehicle. The freedom riders continued their campaign, however, until President John F. Kennedy intervened and directed the enforcement of regulations barring segregation in interstate travel.

The protest movement continued to accelerate as different leaders and groups—buoyed by recent gains—tested new tactics and strategies. Many established community-based projects that sought to combat the barriers that kept blacks from voting. Oth-

NAACP office workers in Detroit organize a membership drive in the 1940s. Members fight to end segregation in housing, education, and public life.

ers targeted the white terrorism that continued to intimidate blacks into submission. In this vein, King and other leaders launched a massive campaign that brought together thousands of blacks in Birmingham, Alabama, one of the most segregated and violently racist cities at the time. Early in the campaign, King was arrested and jailed. From his cell, he penned his famous "Letter from Birmingham Jail," which earned him the support of many sympathetic whites.

Meanwhile, as blacks continued the desegregation campaign in Birmingham, an event occurred that irrevocably commanded the attention of America and its leaders: In an effort to stop a demonstration, the notoriously racist police chief Eugene "Bull" Connor turned vicious attack dogs and fire hoses on the peaceful demonstrators. The force of the water slammed women and children to the ground and sent others hurling through the air. Television coverage and other media reports of these brutal assaults shocked the nation—and viewers around the world. After a month of this highly publicized violence, city officials repealed Birmingham's segregation laws.

In Birmingham's aftermath, mass demonstrations continued to spread, as did fierce resistance within the white community. On June 12, 1963, for example, Alabama governor George Wallace brazenly attempted to block the entrance of two black students to the University of Alabama. Although Wallace was unsuccessful, tempers in the black community flared. That night, President Kennedy addressed the nation in a televised speech. Pledging to align his presidency with the cause of civil rights, Kennedy called for legislation that would ban segregation and broaden the federal protection of civil rights for all Americans.

The March on Washington

In response to these events, King and other leaders, including the veteran civil rights activist A. Philip Randolph, planned a mass gathering on the nation's capital in the summer of 1963. The leaders hoped to spur the passage of civil rights legislation and promote economic opportunity within the black community. On August 28, the March on Washington brought an estimated quarter of a million people, black and white, before the Lincoln Memorial, where King delivered his now famous "I Have a Dream" speech. In rousing words, King described a world of racial harmony and equality:

> I have a dream that my four little children will one day live in a nation where they will not be judged by the color of their skin but by the content of their character. I have a dream today. I have a dream that one day the state of Alabama . . . will be transformed into a situation where little black boys and black girls will be able to join hands with little white boys and white girls and walk together as sisters and brothers. I have a dream today.

The March on Washington generated high hopes that blacks would soon fully realize the dream of America. Black optimism was soon tempered, however. In addition to a spate of highly publicized incidents of racial violence, the much vaunted civil rights legislation seemed to languish in Congress. Following President Kennedy's assassination in November 1963, though, President Lyndon B. Johnson resolved to translate Kennedy's commitment to civil rights into action. After much political maneuvering, Johnson won congressional approval and signed the Civil Rights Act of 1964 into law. The legislation outlawed segregation in public facilities and discrimination in employment and education.

Meanwhile, SNCC had inaugurated a wide-scale campaign to bolster voting rights. To this end, the group launched a massive voter registration drive throughout the South, concentrating on Mississippi, where less than 5 percent of the state's eligible blacks were registered to vote. Freedom Summer, as it became known, was marked by episodes of extreme white terrorism. One of the most heinous examples involved three young civil rights workers. The trio was working to register voters when they were arrested and later murdered by the Ku Klux Klan.

By 1965 the voting campaign had shifted to Selma, Alabama, where, under the leadership of King, thousands of demonstrators began a fifty-mile trek to Montgomery. This time, as the peaceful demonstrators approached the Edmund Pettis Bridge, state troopers used police whips and clubs to halt their progress. The scene blasted into American living rooms via the nightly news. After

"Bloody Sunday," thousands of people reconvened and completed the march, this time under the protection of the Alabama National Guard. On August 6, 1965, shortly after the highly publicized events in Selma, President Johnson signed into law the Voting Rights Act, which, for the first time since Reconstruction, effectively opened up the polls to southern black Americans.

The Rise of Black Nationalism

By the mid-1960s, many black activists started to lose faith in the civil rights reforms that thus far had targeted only the most blatant forms of discrimination. The demise of court-mandated segregation, for example, did not bestow immediate equality upon blacks or reform a political system that left blacks economically and politically crippled. Thus, while King's nonviolent direct-action approach had dominated the 1950s and early 1960s, many blacks, particularly in the North, adopted a more revolutionary stance.

As a wave of nationalist sentiment grew within the movement, organizations such as SNCC and CORE took up more militant agendas. The once moderate SNCC, for example, began advocating a program of "black power"—a term that endorsed racial pride and, in its most extreme form, complete separation from white society.

The greatest spokesman for black nationalism was Malcolm X. With his working-class roots and charismatic style of speaking, Malcolm appealed to a broad band of young urban blacks. Malcolm rejected King's advocacy of nonviolence and instead urged his followers to secure their rights "by any means necessary." The NAACP and SCLC, still striving to integrate into mainstream society, vehemently criticized Malcolm's revolutionary views, and especially his advocacy of complete racial separation. After Malcolm's assassination in February 1965, another extremely provocative black nationalist group emerged: the Black Panthers, a group that boldly adopted the slain leader's mantra "by any means necessary."

Black discontent continued to swell during the latter half of the decade. Race riots exploded across America, as blacks trapped in urban slums lashed out against the poverty and racism still rampant in their communities. Not only did the riots devastate ghetto areas that were home to millions of blacks, including those in the Watts section of Los Angeles, but the racial violence amplified the deepening chasm between those who continued to believe that civil rights could be achieved through peaceful means and the more militant vanguard of the movement. King's assassination in April 1968 dealt perhaps the final crippling blow to the already fractured civil rights movement. Although groups with opposing agendas continued to operate, what had once been a unified quest for civil rights had splintered and lost momentum.

The Legacy of the Civil Rights Movement

The American civil rights movement nevertheless left a permanent mark on American society. The most overt forms of racial discrimination came to an end, and racial violence declined immeasurably. Today, African Americans can freely exercise their right to vote, and in communities where blacks were once barred from the polls, blacks are elected to public offices. Millions of blacks, too, have been lifted out of poverty as a result of the many economic opportunities created by the civil rights movement. Also important, the civil rights movement served as a model for the advancement of other minority groups, including women, the disabled, gays, Hispanics, and many others.

Despite these gains, the civil rights movement fell short on many counts, and the fight for equality is far from over. Yet the black freedom struggle achieved something enduring: It profoundly changed people's attitudes and made the promise of America if not a reality, at least a possibility.

CHAPTER 1

How Did the Fight for Rights Begin?

✹ Chapter Preface

Long before the civil rights movement of the 1950s and 1960s was making headlines, the black response to oppression and racial inequality was well under way. Indeed, while the failed promise of emancipation in the latter half of the nineteenth century gave rise to Jim Crow—a series of laws and customs that segregated and disfranchised blacks—it also compelled a host of individuals to launch efforts to assert their constitutional rights and improve their standing in society. Near the turn of the century, for example, the outspoken crusader Ida B. Wells grappled with one of the leading problems of her day: the lynching of black men. Through a carefully orchestrated journalistic attack, Wells almost singlehandedly brought this form of racial violence—certainly one of the most trenchant symbols of white supremacy—to the forefront of the nation's consciousness. Still others mobilized to create the landmark organizations that would shape and support the fight for rights: Marcus Garvey formed the Universal Negro Improvement Association in 1917 to promote his contention that blacks should work for self-determination, an idea that prefigured the black power movement of the 1960s. Similarly, in 1905, W.E.B. Du Bois and others formed the Niagara Movement to address black grievances, which led to the highly influential National Association for the Advancement of Colored People—and the legal assault on discrimination.

While these early black activists sought a similar prize—a more equitable society—their means and goals were not always unified; in some cases, their efforts to eliminate racial barriers were in direct opposition to one another. For example, Booker T. Washington advocated vocational training and economic independence as a tactical response, in part, to the southern agricultural economy. Washington's pragmatic approach, however, came under fire when he told a predominantly white crowd in 1895, "In all things that are purely social, we can be as separate as the fingers, yet one as the hand in all things essential to mutual progress." Washington's critics, most notably W.E.B. Du Bois, denounced this apparent endorsement of segregation and willingness to forego black political power. Unlike Washington, Du Bois, a Harvard-educated intellectual, advocated the total transformation of black political and cultural life.

The opposing viewpoints represented in the following chapter reflect many of the same debates that would inform and shape the later civil rights movement. At the same time, they show how a cadre of dedicated individuals, despite a profusion of tactical and ideological differences, set the stage for the all-out assault against inequality that transformed the racial landscape of America.

Viewpoint 1

"The wisest among my race understand that the agitation of questions of social equality is the extremest folly."

Blacks Should Not Agitate for Civil Rights

Booker T. Washington

Born a slave on a Virginia plantation, Booker T. Washington rose to become one of the most influential black leaders of the late nineteenth and early twentieth centuries. Early in his career, Washington founded the Tuskegee Institute, a vocational school that promoted industrial education and self-improvement as a means of uplifting blacks. Yet it was Washington's 1895 address before the Atlanta Exposition that catapulted the renowned educator into the national spotlight. His speech, reprinted here, became one of the most influential—and controversial—addresses in American history.

Responding to the rise of Jim Crow, a system of laws and customs that disfranchised blacks, Washington, speaking before a biracial audience, advocates a policy of accommodation on racial issues, urging blacks to forego political and legal action in

Booker T. Washington, speech at the Atlanta Exposition, September 18, 1895.

favor of vocational training and work in industry. While many praised Washington's practical approach to racial problems, critics soon emerged. Foremost of those to challenge Washington's "Atlanta Compromise" was W.E.B. Du Bois, who found that it compromised social equality by accommodating a deeply entrenched system of racism.

M r. President and Gentlemen of the Board of Directors and Citizens:

One-third of the population of the South is of the Negro race. No enterprise seeking the material, civil, or moral welfare of this section can disregard this element of our population and reach the highest success. I but convey to you, Mr. President and Directors, the sentiment of the masses of my race when I say that in no way have the value and manhood of the American Negro been more fittingly and generously recognized than by the managers of this magnificent exposition at every stage of its progress. It is a recognition that will do more to cement the friendship of the two races than any occurrence since the dawn of our freedom. Not only this, but the opportunity here afforded will awaken among us a new era of industrial progress. Ignorant and inexperienced, it is not strange that in the first years of our new life we began at the top instead of at the bottom; that a seat in Congress or the state legislature was more sought than real estate or industrial skill; that the political convention or stump speaking had more attractions than starting a dairy farm or truck garden.

A ship lost at sea for many days suddenly sighted a friendly vessel. From the mast of the unfortunate vessel was seen a signal: "Water, water; we die of thirst!" The answer from the friendly vessel at once came back: "Cast down your bucket where you are." A second time the signal, "Water, water, send us water!" ran up from the distressed vessel, and was answered: "Cast down your bucket where you are." And a third and fourth signal for water was answered: "Cast down your bucket where you are."

The captain of the distressed vessel, at last heeding the injunction, cast down his bucket, and it came up full of fresh, sparkling water from the mouth of the Amazon River. To those of my race who depend on bettering their condition in a foreign land or who underestimate the importance of cultivating friendly relations with the Southern white man, who is their next-door neighbor, I would say: Cast down your bucket where you are; cast it down in making friends, in every manly way, of the people of all races by whom we are surrounded. Cast it down in agriculture, mechanics, in commerce, in domestic service, and in the professions. And in this connection it is well to bear in mind that whatever other sins the South may be called to bear, when it comes to business, pure and simple, it is in the South that the Negro is given a man's chance in the commercial world, and in nothing is this exposition more eloquent than in emphasizing this chance.

Our greatest danger is that, in the great leap from slavery to freedom, we may overlook the fact that the masses of us are to live by the productions of our hands and fail to keep in mind that we shall prosper in proportion as we learn to dignify and glorify common labor, and put brains and skill into the common occupations of life; shall prosper in proportion as we learn to draw the line between the superficial and the substantial, the ornamental gewgaws of life and the useful. No race can prosper till it learns that there is as much dignity in tilling a field as in writing a poem. It is at the bottom of life we must begin, and not at the top. Nor should we permit our grievances to overshadow our opportunities.

To those of the white race who look to the incoming of those of foreign birth and strange tongue and habits for the prosperity of the South, were I permitted I would repeat what I say to my own race, "Cast down your bucket where you are." Cast it down among the 8 million Negroes whose habits you know, whose fidelity and love you have tested in days when to have proved treacherous meant the ruin of your firesides. Cast down your bucket among these people who have, without strikes and labor wars, tilled your fields, cleared your forests, builded your railroads and cities, and brought forth treasures from the bowels of the earth and helped make possible this magnificent representation of the progress of the South. Casting down your bucket among my people, helping and encouraging them as you are doing on these grounds, and, with education of head, hand, and heart, you will find that they will buy your surplus land, make blossom the waste places in your fields, and run your factories.

While doing this, you can be sure in the future, as in the past, that you and your families will be surrounded by the most patient, faithful, law-abiding, and unresentful people that the world has seen. As we have proved our loyalty to you in the past, in nursing your children, watching by the sickbed of your mothers and fathers, and often following them with tear-dimmed eyes to their graves, so in the future, in our humble way, we shall stand by you with a devotion that no foreigner can approach, ready to lay down our lives, if need be, in defense of yours; interlacing our industrial, commercial, civil, and religious life with yours in a way that shall make the interests of both races one. In all things that are purely social we can be as separate as the fingers, yet one as the hand in all things essential to mutual progress.

Development for All

There is no defense or security for any of us except in the highest intelligence and development of all. If anywhere there are efforts tending to curtail the fullest growth of the Negro, let these efforts be turned into stimulating, encouraging, and making him the most useful and intelligent citizen. Effort or means so invested will pay a thousand percent interest. These efforts will be twice blessed—"blessing him that gives and him that takes."

There is no escape, through law of man or God, from the inevitable:

The laws of changeless justice bind
Oppressor with oppressed;
And dose as sin and suffering joined
We march to fate abreast

Nearly 16 millions of hands will aid you in pulling the load upward, or they will pull against you the load downward. We shall constitute one-third and more of the ignorance and crime of the South, or one-third its intelligence and progress; we shall contribute one-third to the business and industrial prosperity of the South, or we shall prove a veritable body of death, stagnating, depressing, retarding every effort to advance the body politic.

Gentlemen of the exposition, as we present to you our humble effort at an exhibition of our progress, you must not expect over-much. Starting thirty years ago with ownership here and there in a few quilts and pumpkins and chickens (gathered from miscellaneous sources), remember: the path that has led from these to the invention and production of agricultural implements, buggies, steam engines, newspapers, books, statuary, carving, paintings, the management of drugstores and banks, has not been trodden without contact with thorns and thistles. While we take pride in what we exhibit as a result of our independent efforts, we do not for a moment forget that our part in this exhibition would fall far short of your expectations but for the constant help that has come to our educational life, not only from the Southern states but especially from Northern philanthropists who have made their gifts a constant stream of blessing and encouragement.

The wisest among my race understand that the agitation of questions of social equality is the extremest folly, and that progress in the enjoyment of all the privileges that will come to us must be the result of severe and constant struggle rather than of artificial forcing. No race that has anything to contribute to the markets of the world is long in any degree ostracized. It is important and right that all privileges of the law be ours, but it is vastly more important that we be prepared for the exercise of these privileges. The opportunity to earn a dollar in a factory just now is worth infinitely more than the opportunity to spend a dollar in an opera house.

A Pledge to Cooperate

In conclusion, may I repeat that nothing in thirty years has given us more hope and encouragement and drawn us so near to you of the white race as this opportunity offered by the exposition; and here bending, as it were, over the altar that represents the results of the struggles of your race and mine, both starting practically empty-handed three decades ago, I pledge that, in your effort to work out the great and intricate problem which God has laid at the doors of the South, you shall have at all times the patient, sympathetic help of my race; only let this be constantly in mind that, while from representations in these buildings of the product of field, of forest, of mine, of factory, letters, and art, much good will come—yet far above and beyond material benefits will be that higher good, that let us pray God will come, in a blotting out of sectional differences and racial animosities and suspicions, in a determination to administer absolute justice, in a willing obedience among all classes to the mandates of law. This, coupled with our material prosperity, will bring into our beloved South a new heaven and a new earth.

Viewpoint 2

"If we remember the history of all great reform movements, we remember that they have been preceded by agitation."

Blacks Should Agitate for Civil Rights

W.E.B. Du Bois

As the black freedom struggle was gaining strength at the turn of the century, W.E.B. Du Bois was well on his way to becoming the nation's preeminent black intellectual and spokesperson. Born a free black man just after the end of the Civil War, Du Bois became the first black man to graduate from Harvard and went on to help found the influential National Association for the Advancement of Colored People (NAACP) and the organization's widely read journal, the *Crisis*.

A prolific scholar and outspoken political leader, Du Bois exposed the black experience perhaps more profoundly than any leader of his day. In his writings and speeches, Du Bois not only pointed out the social and psychological ramifications of racial injustice, but also advocated vigorous protest as a means of advancing social equality—an approach that ran counter to Booker T. Washington's accommodation strategy. In the following 1907 speech, Du Bois, who viewed accommodation as acquiescence in blacks' second-class citizenship, explains why agitation is a powerful weapon in the fight for black rights.

W.E.B. Du Bois, speech, *The Voice of the Negro*, vol. 4, March 1907.

There are those people in the world who object to agitation and one cannot wholly blame them. Agitation, after all, is unpleasant. It means that while you are going peaceably and joyfully on your way some half-mad person insists upon saying things that you do not like to hear. They may be true, but you do not like to hear them. You would rather wait till some convenient season; or you take up your newspaper and instead of finding pleasant notices about your friends and the present progress of the world, you read of some restless folks who insist on talking about wrong and crime and unpleasant things. It would be much better if we did not have to have agitation; if we had a world where everything was going so well and it was unnecessary often to protest strongly, even wildly, of the evil and the wrong of the universe. As a matter of fact, however, no matter how unpleasant the agitator is, and no matter how inconvenient and unreasonable his talk, yet we must ever have him with us. And why? Because this is a world where things are not all right. We are gifted with human nature, which does not do the right or even desire the right always. So long as these things are true, then we are faced by this dilemma: either we must let the evil alone and refuse to hear of it or listen to it or we must try and right it. Now, very often it happens that the evil is there, the wrong has been done, and yet we do not hear of it—we do not know about it. Here then comes the agitator. He is the herald—he is the prophet—he is the man that says to the world: "There are evils which you do not know; but which I know, and you must listen to them." Now, of course, there may be agitators who are telling the truth and there may be agitators who are telling untruths. Those who are not telling the truth may be lying or they may be mistaken. So that agitation in itself does not necessarily mean always the right and always reform.

Here, then, is some one who thinks that he has discovered some dangerous evil and wants to call the attention of good men of the world to it. If he does not persevere, we may perhaps pass him by. If he is easily discouraged, we may perhaps think that the evil which he thought he saw has been cured. But if he is sincere and if he is persistent, then there is but one thing for a person to do who wants to live in a world worth living in; that is, listen to him carefully, prove his tale and then try and right the wrong.

Other Reform Movements

If we remember the history of all great reform movements, we remember that they have been preceded by agitation. Take, for instance, the suppression of the slave trade. It was in a day when slavery could not be successfully attacked. But there was no doubt of the horrors of the slave trade. The best and worst of people alike admitted that. Here came a young man just graduated from college. By writing a prize essay he found himself interested in this great evil. He began to know and learn of things which other people did not know. Not that they knew nothing about them, but they had not brought together all the facts. One isolated person knew that fact and one knew this fact, but no one person knew both facts in juxtaposition. When they did become acquainted with all the facts he was sure that they must be moved to act. What then must he do? He must agitate. It was not pleasant—it was putting himself in jeopardy; he was called upon to lose friends in some cases, and in all cases to make himself unpleasant, insistent, persistent, telling of things that people did not want to hear about, because they were not interested in them. He must interest people in things in which they were not interested before, which is a hard task in this busy world; and yet, nevertheless, if [Thomas] Clarkson [pioneer British abolitionist] had not persisted, we would have much less than a chance to agitate for human rights today.

So it is with all great movements. They must be preceded by agitation. In the present status of the Negro it is particularly necessary that we today make the world realize what his position is—make them realize that he is not merely insisting on ornamental rights, and neglecting plain duties, but that the rights we want are the rights that are necessary, inevitable before we can rightly do our duties.

Mrs. [Charlotte] Gilman [an influential suffragist and reformer] has a poem somewhere, where she speaks of that rule which is to be laid down in the great future state, "Unless a man works, he may not eat," and she says very aptly that "the cart is before the horse," because "unless a man eats he cannot work." So to those people who are saying to black men today, "Do your duties first, and then clamor for rights," we have a right to answer and to answer insistently, that the rights we are clamoring for are those that will enable us to do our duties. That we cannot possibly be asked to do any partial measure of our duty even, unless we can have those rights and have them now. We realize this. The great mass of people in the United States do not realize it. What then are we to do? We may sit in courteous and dumb self-forgetting silence until other people are interested and come to our rescue. But is it reasonable to suppose that this is going to happen before degeneration and destruction overtake us? This is a busy world. People are attending to their own affairs as they ought to. The man that has a grievance is supposed to speak for himself. No one can speak for him—no one knows the thing as well as he does. Therefore it is reasonable to say that if the man does not complain that it is because he has no complaint. If a man does not express his needs, then it is because his needs are filled. And it has been our great mistake in the last decade that we have been silent and still and have not complained when it was our duty not merely to ourselves but to our country and to humanity in general to complain and to complain loudly. It is, then, high time that the Negro agitator should be heard in the land.

It is not a pleasant role to play. It is not always pleasant to nice ears to hear a man ever coming with his dark facts and unpleasant conditions. Nevertheless it is the highest optimism to bring forward the dark side of any human picture. When a man does this he says to the world, "Things are bad, but it is worthwhile to let the world know that things are bad in order that they may become better." The real crushing pessimism takes hold of the world when people say things are so bad that they are not worth complaining of, because they cannot be made better.

Complain Loudly

It is manifest that within the last year the whole race in the United States has awakened to the fact that they have lost ground and must start complaining and complain loudly. It is their business to complain.

This complaint should be made with reason and with strict regard to the truth, but nevertheless it should be made. And it is interesting to find even those persons who were deriding complaint a few years ago joining in the agitation today.

We of Niagara Movement [a civil rights protest organization founded in 1905 and the direct forerunner of the National Association for the Advancement of Colored People (NAACP)] welcome them. We are glad of help from all sources. We are confirmed in our belief that if a man stand up and tell the thing he wants and point out the evil around him, that this is the best way to get rid of it. May we not hope, then, that we are going to have in the next century a solid front on the part of colored people in the United States saying we want education for our children and we do not have it today in any large measure; we want full political rights, and we never have had that; we want to be treated as human beings; and we want those of our race who stand on the threshold and within the veil of crime to be treated not as beasts, but as men who can be reformed or as children who can be prevented from going further in their career.

If we all stand and demand this insistently, the nation must listen to the voice of ten millions.

Viewpoint 3

*"This Washington brand of black leadership would
. . . neglect the quest for full-fledged citizenship
status and human rights."*

Booker T. Washington's Leadership Was Flawed

Martin Kilson

As one of the nation's chief black spokespersons, Booker
T. Washington stood at the forefront of race relations in
nineteenth-century America. In his assessment of post-
Reconstruction race leadership, Martin Kilson contends that
Washington engendered only miniscule black advancement.
Instead, Washington too narrowly focused on social system development, or rather bolstering those agencies, networks, and
institutions that would spur black social development. According to Kilson, this strategy was ineffective not only because it
failed to address the second-class citizenship status and human
rights parity of African Americans, but also because it relied too
heavily on the role of whites in bestowing economic and educational opportunity. Martin Kilson is a research professor at Har-

Martin Kilson, "The Washington and Du Bois Leadership Paradigms Recon-
sidered," *The Annals of the American Academy of Political and Social Science*,
vol. 568, March 2000. Copyright © 2000 by Sage Publications, Inc. Reproduced by permission.

vard University and the author and coauthor of several books, including *The Making of Black Intellectuals: Studies on the African American Intelligentsia.* The following viewpoint is excerpted from an article that originally appeared in the *Annals of the American Academy of Political and Social Science.*

One function [of leadership] can be characterized by the term that anthropologists often use—social organization. That is, leadership is concerned with fashioning the nuts and bolts of a social system, the infrastructure of agencies and networks that allow individuals and a people as a whole to realize the purposes required for a viable human existence. Thus, one core type of leadership we can call social organization type leadership.

A second function of leadership is to offer guidance and goals for a community, to direct a community to certain ends and purposes. This leadership function is concerned with a group's status, rights, and honor. This second core type of leadership we can call guidance type or mobilization type leadership. It is from this second type of leadership in a modern nation-state society that political leadership evolves, whether activist or social movement leadership or elected politician leadership.

In general, for African Americans the end of Reconstruction and the imposition of racial caste marginalization of black citizens in American society placed a barrier to the natural growth of guidance or mobilization type leadership. Within the South, where the vast majority of African Americans resided between the 1890s and the 1950s, mobilization type leadership was extremely limited, aggressively restricted by the authoritarian white racist patterns. For example, by 1940 only 5 percent of the adult black population in the South had been allowed to become registered voters. White violence and white bureaucratic coercion were employed to impose this lowest level participation ceiling on African American citizens.

As a result, a massive federal government intervention was required to alter this situation (which finally came with the Voting Rights Act of 1965), and meanwhile the majority community of African Americans in the South had to resort to that more primary (or embryonic) form of leadership that I call social organization leadership. Indeed, a variant of social organization leadership was articulated along systemic lines by the most prominent African American political figure in the South from the late 1880s to his death in 1915. That figure was Booker T. Washington.

The Washington Leadership Paradigm

If we could magically transport ourselves back 100 years or so to Atlanta, Georgia, in 1895, we would have experienced an extraordinary event. That event would shape the metamorphosis of African American leadership processes—and thus the processes of black political incorporation in American life—for the first four generations of the twentieth century.

The extraordinary event I refer to was the presence of Booker T. Washington at a capitalist industrial exposition. As a keynote speaker at the 1895 Atlanta Exposition, Washington told an audience of white entrepreneurs—the leading figures of an exploding American industrial capitalism—that all they had to worry about in regard to a troublesome American working class was the white working class. As Washington was well aware, the white

Influential civil rights leader Booker T. Washington addresses a large crowd. Many of Washington's colleagues criticized his strategy on black advancement.

working class had or could bid for full citizenship status (they were within the American social contract) and thus could participate in helping to define the emergent industrial nation-state's public purposes.

But what about the black working class? Above all, the black working class was outside the American social contract—and brutally outside it at that. Most (over 90 percent) of the African American working class was an oppressed agrarian proletariat whom historians, cognizant of its dilapidated attributes, labeled a peonage agrarian class. In other words, the African American working class was not just overwhelmed by massive social oppression but overwhelmed as well by judicial, police, and political oppression. The cruelest kind of systemic oppression under capitalism was endured by the southern branch of the black working class—perhaps one-third of whom faced the horrible experience of prison labor under vicious white superintendence from the 1890s to the 1950s, or, nearly as bad, they experienced the terrible threat of imprisonment for the purpose of becoming prison labor.

Booker T. Washington's message to the assembled industrial capitalists was at the other end of the political spectrum from what that young African American who was just finishing his doctorate at Harvard University in 1895—W.E.B. Du Bois—would have told the Atlanta Exposition participants had he been invited to it. In direct reference to that core query—how do you lead black people?—Booker T. Washington's Atlanta Exposition speech belittled the possibility of using politics to advance African American needs, concerns, and status in a raucously evolving industrial capitalism. He said, "Start . . . a dairy farm or truck garden" instead. Raising his two hands, Washington proclaimed that, in matters of political rights and status, whites and blacks would be as "separate as the fingers on my hands." In short, Washington's address rejected the guidance type or mobilization type leadership model, favoring instead the social organization type leadership model.

The Role of Whites

From these groundwork propositions, then, Washington sought to strike a bargain with America's captains of industry and, through them, with America's operational authoritarian white supremacist overrule of some 10 million black people. Washington opined that if the white elites and leadership would funnel financial and institutional resources to what I call his social organization type black leadership, this Washington brand of black leadership would, on one hand, advance the African American social system while, on the other hand, neglect the quest for full-fledged citizenship status and human rights—rights that were by 1895 some 30 years old, enshrined in the Constitution on pain of a bloody Civil War and elaborated by federal legislation known as the Civil Rights Codes of 1865, 1866, and 1867. In *The Future of the American Negro*, Booker T. Washington presents his accommodationist formulations:

> I believe the past and present teach but one lesson—to the Negro's [white] friends and to the Negro himself—that there is but one hope of solution; and that is for the Negro in every part of America to resolve from henceforth that he will throw aside every non-essential [citizenship and human rights] and cling only to essential—that his pillar of fire by night and pillar of cloud by day shall be property, economy, education, and Christian character. To us just now these are the wheat, all else the chaff.

There was in Washington's accommodationist schema no timetable for the establishment of African American citizenship and human rights parity. Gunnar Myrdal's classic appraisal of African American citizenship status as of the middle 1940s states that, "Through thrift, skill, and industry the Negroes were gradually to improve so much that, at a later stage, the discussion again could be taken up concerning his rights. This was Washington's philosophy."

Booker T. Washington was not, of course, a simpleton. He knew that if he could get the American elites in 1895 to generate financial and material resources to advance blacks in education, job opportunities, and neighborhood development, this very process of social system development would inevitably converge with the American political system. He also knew that, given his autocratic leadership style, he would be the top client type or errand boy black leadership figure.

Alas, even though the American elites of the nineteenth and early twentieth centuries with whom Washington interacted never even approximated generating the material resources for African American modernization that Washington's compromise formula implied, Washington nevertheless evolved to that unique and curious role as top client type black leader. So whatever the inadequate supply of financial and material resources from white elites for African American modernization was, Booker T. Washington exercised an inordinate sway over its allocation among blacks.

Washington's top client type black leader role also saw him functioning as the main advisor among African American leadership to President Theodore Roosevelt and President William Taft on those torturous issues related to blacks' authoritarian-delineated interface with the American social contract.

What were the salient political issues requiring Washington's advice? (1) voting rights or rather the steady and cynical disenfranchisement of African Americans well into the twentieth century; (2) pervasive institutional discrimination and/or segregation toward blacks throughout American life; and (3) massive, pernicious violence against blacks generally and against any particular black citizen the perpetrators of white supremacist violence wished to target. Such violence was often taken to the point of taking a black life, by mob lynching or police brutality, the wretched tale of which is related more effectively in Gunnar Myrdal's *An American Dilemma* (1944) than in many other sources.

A Failed Bargain

Thus, what historians have labeled the accommodationist leadership method of Booker T. Washington produced at best sparse and problematic social system advancement—social organization metamorphosis—for the typical African American citizen by, say, World War I. At the time of Washington's death in 1915, over 90 percent of the 11 million blacks in the United States were still massively poor. The so-called bargain that Washington struck with white elites in regard to opening up industrial job markets for the black working class was an utter failure because the white capitalist class made no serious effort to incorporate African American workers at parity with white workers. Neither was the other half of

Washington's so-called bargain with white elites any more successful—the goal of educating the illiterate offspring of slaves through the special financial and resource assistance of white elites. The bulk of the southern black population remained wretchedly educated by the 1930s.

Finally, while full credit belongs to Booker T. Washington for his important contributions to the development of the African American professional class or intelligentsia—with Washington himself founding a key black institution of higher education, Tuskegee Institute—this important class within the African American social system was minuscule at the time of Washington's death in 1915. Nor was the black professional stratum any more fulsome by the start of World War II, mainly because the white elites in general and the white capitalist class in particular failed to keep its pathetic Faustian bargain with Booker T. Washington that commenced with his Atlanta Exposition address in 1895.

In opting for the social organization type black leadership, Washington painted himself and African Americans generally into a leadership cul-de-sac. And had Washington lived perhaps one more generation, the devastating impact of his leadership cul-de-sac in regard to constraining the growth of the guidance type or mobilization type black leadership would have been unbearable.

Viewpoint 4

"[Washington] addressed the most pressing needs of black Southerners and showed them a way of coping with their situation, and even prospering, in a climate of extreme racism."

Booker T. Washington's Leadership Was Effective

Adam Fairclough

Civil rights scholar Adam Fairclough hails Booker T. Washington as a successful and farsighted leader who, whatever his limitations, remained committed to racial equality and ultimately engendered conditions that promoted black progress. Washington's Tuskegee Institute, for example, was an impressive symbol of black gains—and not a repressive machine that kept blacks mired in second-class citizenry. Too, Washington's attempts to dismantle racism by making blacks indispensable to the southern economy—a strategy bitterly criticized by many of his contemporaries—was indeed relevant to Washington's time as it specifically addressed the needs of the South's agricultural industry.

In his final analysis, Fairclough concludes that Washington

has been judged too harshly by his critics. Despite his apparent endorsement of segregation and his refusal to agitate, Washington was not an exemplar of white racist complicity as is so often charged; rather, he offered a beacon of hope to otherwise disfranchised blacks as he paved the way for future civil rights advances. Fairclough has written extensively on the civil rights era. He is the author of *Better Day Coming: Blacks and Equaltiy, 1890–2000*, from which the following is excerpted.

Born in a squalid cabin in Virginia in 1856, the son of a white man whose identity he never knew, Booker Taliaferro Washington was a legendary American success story: his autobiography, *Up from Slavery*, has never been out of print. Through sheer ability and force of character, Washington lifted himself from the depths of bondage to the pinnacle of world fame. A living refutation of America's degrading image of black people, he created Tuskegee Institute, a black school in Alabama that symbolized the achievement and potential of his race. In addition, his unflagging efforts to mend the rift between black and white earned him the reputation of statesman as well as educator. Between 1895, the date of his famous speech to the Atlanta Cotton States and Industrial Exposition, and 1915, the year of his death, Washington was the most powerful black leader in America.

The Atlanta Compromise

In his Atlanta Exposition address, Washington proposed a new settlement between the races in the South. Economic cooperation, he argued, should supersede political conflict. He asked for just treatment from white Southerners and offered two concessions on behalf of his fellow blacks.

Washington's first concession was the admission that Radical Reconstruction had been a mistake. Blacks had started freedom "at the top instead of at the bottom," devoting too much energy to politics and neglecting the skills and habits of industry that would enable them to earn a decent living. The second concession to white opinion was an assurance that blacks were not at all interested in "social equality." What social equality meant was not clear, but it obviously included intermarriage and sexual relations, and many whites read it as a general endorsement of racial segregation. Having verbally eliminated the basic causes of racial antagonism—apart from racism itself, to which he referred in only the most oblique terms—Washington put forward a positive program for economic cooperation. He urged blacks to stay in the South, concentrate on working hard rather than agitating for their rights, and cultivate "friendly relations with the Southern white man." Whites, for their part, should regard blacks as an economic asset rather than a political threat, according them fair treatment as loyal workers. If whites treated blacks justly instead of oppressing them, Washington promised, "we shall stand by you with a devotion that no foreigner can match." If blacks and whites worked together, while at the same time acknowledging each other's racial integrity, the South's economic prosperity would be assured, and both races would share in it. "In all things that are purely social we can be as separate as the fingers, yet as one hand in all things essential to mutual progress."

Hailed by both races as an expression of farsighted wisdom, Washington's "Atlanta Compromise" marked the beginning of a new era in race relations. However, as the nineteenth century gave way to the twentieth, and the oppression of black people did not abate, Washington became the object of bitter censure by a small but influential black minority. The Atlanta Compromise, these critics charged, was not a compromise at all: blacks made all the concessions and whites gave nothing in return. Indeed, because the Atlanta Compromise appeared to usher in the consolidation of white supremacy, some charged that Washington had betrayed the Negro race to its enemies.

That judgment was far too harsh. Whatever his limitations, Washington struggled with great energy and integrity to keep alive the ideal of racial equality at a time when blacks were being subjected to the most intensive ideological assault on their humanity that they had ever experienced. His persistent and largely futile campaign to persuade whites to spell "Negro" with a capital "N" typified his insistence that black people deserved respect. So did his refusal, when he controlled the *New York Age*, to carry advertisements for hair straighteners and skin lighteners. However much Washington compromised in politics, he never conceded the arguments of white racists.

Although some white Southerners heaped praise upon Washington, others suspected that he was a Trojan Horse for racial equality. Many were outraged when Washington dined with President Theodore Roosevelt at the White House in 1901. The incident betrayed Washington's "deep down antipathy to white supremacy," complained an Arkansas schools superintendent. "Afar off he sees a vision of equality," warned Ben Tillman of South Carolina. "The action of President Roosevelt in entertaining that nigger will necessitate our killing a thousand niggers in the South before they will learn their place again."

Such comments contained a basic insight. Washington's ethic of hard work, self-improvement, and Christian morality may strike us as apolitical and excessively individualistic, yet those very virtues, Washington believed, would "give the lie to the assertion of his enemies North and South that the Negro is the inferior of the white man." The average Negro child, he insisted, was the intellectual equal of the average white child. In his autobiography Washington struck a note of almost defiant moral superiority:

> From any point of view, I had rather be what I am, a member of the Negro race, than be able to claim membership with the most favoured of any other race. I have always been made sad when I have heard members of any race claiming rights and privileges . . . on the ground simply that they were members of this or that race, regardless of their own individual worth or attainments. . . . Every persecuted individual and race should get much consolation out of the great human law, which is universal and eternal, that merit, no matter under what skin found, is, in the long run, recognized and rewarded. This I have said here, not to call attention to myself as an individual, but to the race to which I am proud to belong.

Washington's own attainments defied the conventional wisdom that black people were inherently inferior.

Washington's fame, as well as his strategy for black progress, rested upon Tuskegee Institute and the idea it represented. Tuskegee Institute was an impressive achievement. Arriving in Alabama in 1881, Washington transformed a few tumble-down shacks in an Alabama field into a gleaming school of solid red brick (the bricks were fired by the students themselves in Tuskegee's own kiln). A tireless fundraiser who spent several months each year on the road cultivating Northern benefactors, he built up a $2 million endowment and acquired thousands of acres of land for the school.

Tuskegee Institute was staffed and administered entirely by black people: Washington insisted upon it. "I knew that . . . we were trying an experiment—that of testing whether or not it was possible for Negroes to build up and control the affairs of a large educational institution." In creating a black-run school, Washington made a statement about racial equality that was far more powerful than words. "Tuskegee alone is the fruit of a black man's heart and brain and effort and administrative skill," wrote Roscoe Conkling Bruce, one of its teachers. "Tuskegee Institute is . . . proof of the black man's capacity for the tasks of civilization." Washington made Tuskegee Institute the most famous Negro school in the world. To black people in America, and to black Africans and West Indians as well, Tuskegee was a proud symbol of what their race could achieve. It was a beacon of hope.

Tuskegee was more than a school: it also represented a philosophy of racial progress through education. The "Tuskegee Idea" was this: The vast majority of blacks were not going to better their position by means of politics, protest, or higher learning. Their salvation lay in mastering basic work skills and applying them, with honest sweat, to the demands of the South's agricultural economy. Four-fifths of the South's black population lived in the rural areas; most of them farmed white-owned land as renters or sharecroppers. Whatever their hardships and problems, therefore, blacks in the South began life with one inestimable advantage: Whites needed their labor. Building upon this foundation, they would be able to pull themselves up by their own bootstraps. Washington envisaged them becoming landowners, artisans, and small businessmen.

In stressing the economic opportunities available to blacks who worked hard and possessed the right skills, Washington persistently downplayed white racism. Yes, he told a New York audience in 1890, he knew all about lynching, ballot-box stuffing, and intimidation: the reports were "generally true." But he pointed to "an absence of prejudice against the colored man in the South in the matter of business that counts for a great deal." Blacks could utilize white self-interest as the "entering wedge" to equality. If they proved themselves to be loyal, willing, and efficient workers, if they made themselves indispensable to the Southern economy, whites would respect them and treat them fairly. Blacks would erode white prejudice just as the action of water makes rough stones smooth. In time, whites would willingly accord them full citizenship rights, including the right to vote.

"Industrial education," Washington believed, would best prepare blacks for surviving and prospering in the New South. As applied to the education of freedmen by Washington's mentor, Samuel Chapman Armstrong, the former missionary and Union general who founded Hampton Institute in Virginia, industrial education meant teaching practical skills in agriculture and the "mechanic arts" that would equip blacks to earn a living in the rural South. The regime at Hampton Institute, and later at Tuskegee Institute, required all students to perform manual labor about the school: cooking, cleaning, farming, printing, building, gardening, and so on. Such labor enabled Washington to build and maintain Tuskegee on the cheap, and helped impecunious students to work their way through school. But manual labor also served a higher moral purpose: "The students themselves would be taught to see not only utility in labour, but beauty and dignity; would be taught . . . how to lift labour up from mere drudgery and toil, and would learn to love work for its own sake." Industrial education did not train blacks to enter industry, but rather taught them to be industrious. To reinforce this character-building mission, both Hampton and Tuskegee subjected students to strict rules and military-style discipline.

Hampton and Tuskegee deliberately distinguished themselves from the many colleges and universities established in the South after the Civil War by Northern churches and missionary societies. Although these institutions had done pioneering work in educating the freedmen, and had trained the first generation of Southern black teachers, they were ill-suited to the needs of the black population as a whole. In reality, the black universities were mainly elementary and secondary schools, with only a handful of students taking college-level courses. Yet, emulating the colleges of New England, they laid great stress on the classics, modern languages, and other staples of nineteenth-century higher education. Many whites, and some blacks, criticized the black universities for being pretentious and overambitious, complaining that their rarefied curriculum equipped blacks to be teachers, preachers, and politicians, but had little to offer the toiling masses. It had been folly to begin "at the apex of the educational fabric instead of at the base," wrote T. Thomas Fortune in 1884; money had been lavished on black colleges when "ordinary common schools were unknown." Blacks in the South were most in need of elementary and individual education—"preparation for the actual work of life." Hampton and Tuskegee attempted to fill that need. Pointedly, they did not teach Latin or Greek, nor did they offer degrees.

Washington's Opponents

A host of black critics, and generations of historians, have lamented Washington's influence over black education. Samuel Chapman Armstrong, they argue, conceived of industrial education as a means of adjusting blacks to a subordinate position in the New South. "He believed that blacks should be taught to remain in their place," writes historian Donald Spivey, to "stay out of politics, keep quiet about their rights, and work." Industrial education meant, in practice, training blacks for nothing better than low-grade, low-paid jobs, equipping them to be cooks, servants, sharecroppers, and laborers—the "hewers of wood and drawers of waters" so beloved of Southern whites. True, Hampton Institute trained its students to be teachers, not farmers or laborers; so did Tuskegee Institute. By molding black teachers, however, Armstrong attempted to mold the black masses. Booker T. Washington, his star pupil, absorbed his ideas and perpetuated them at Tuskegee, which trained further cohorts of conservative teachers. Spivey likened Washington to the black slave-driver who, "given the position of authority over his fellow slaves, worked diligently to keep intact the very system under which they both were enslaved."

What angered Washington's opponents was not so much the

idea of "industrial education" itself—there was widespread agreement that black children would benefit from being taught practical skills—as the fear that blacks would be denied all but the most rudimentary schooling, thereby perpetuating their second-class citizenship. Washington vigorously denied that he sought to place a ceiling upon black achievement. Yet his white supporters viewed industrial education in precisely that way, and they used Washington's ideas to justify a dual standard of education: a superior one for whites and a grossly inferior one for blacks.

Washington disclaimed any hostility to higher education for blacks, explaining simply that the great mass of the black population required elementary and secondary school of a practical bent. . . .

Washington's Achievements

His most thorough biographer, Louis Harlan, portrayed Washington as a master manipulator whose relentless pursuit of power, and skill at disguising his real emotions and opinions, produced spiritual emptiness and political corruption. Washington emerges from Harlan's pages as a despotic, devious, and rather sinister figure—and above all as a failure. "Seeking to be all things to all men . . . Washington 'jumped Jim Crow' with the skill of long practice, but he seemed to lose sight of his dance."

However, the Washington that looms across the massive bulk of his collected papers—which, ironically, Harlan himself edited—is an altogether different character. As historian Virginia Denton has argued, far from showing a power-obsessed enigma, Washington's letters and speeches disclose a man unselfishly committed to the social, educational, and economic uplift of his race. "Washington was dominated by purpose, not power," Judged by his best, Washington was an admirable leader. He addressed the most pressing needs of black Southerners and showed them a way of coping with their situation, and even prospering, in a climate of extreme racism. Using a combination of flattery, persuasion, and guile, he gradually wore down Southern white opposition to black education. When blacks in the South were abandoned by the Republican Party, Washington built alliances with Northern capitalists and philanthropists. His much-criticized relationship with President Roosevelt important symbolic value, for it told Southern blacks that they had a foot in the White House door. Washington's economic vision strikes us as unrealistic. At a time of pellmell urbanization, Washington urged blacks to stay in the countryside. In an age of breakneck industrialization, he envisaged blacks as yeoman farmers, self-employed artisans, and independent entrepreneurs. At the time, however, Washington's message did not seem irrelevant. To the emerging black middle class of teachers and small businessmen it was an inspiration. To black farmers, it offered a road map out of tenancy and debt. Indeed, by 1900, about one black farmer in four—some 193,000 people—were landowners. They achieved this, moreover, despite Congress's refusal to apportion land to the freedmen, despite the obstacle of discrimination, and despite a credit system hat made it extremely difficult to accumulate capital. This golden age of agriculture did not last. Even at its height, blacks, who comprised 28 percent of the South's farmers, accounted for only 14 percent of the region's farm owners. Moreover, the era of the small farmer was drawing to a close. Washington failed to predict how economic change, abetted by government policy, would completely transform American agriculture. Still, he was hardly the only person who lacked a crystal ball. Not even the experts predicted that most farmers, white as well as black, would be swept from the land in a matter of decades.

Washington's reputation as a Victorian moralist who constantly berated blacks for their shortcomings still persists. His priorities were hardly misplaced, however. Washington sought to raise the standards of people who had been denied legal marriage, refused education, clothed in rags, and housed in squalor. His seeming obsession with cleanliness, for example—famously exemplified by his praise of the toothbrush as a civilizing influence—strikes us today as ridiculous. In the context of his age, however, such concerns were not so absurd. Reformers on both sides of the Atlantic were vitally interested in sanitation and public health. Black Americans suffered an especially high mortality rate: eliminating dirt meant eliminating disease. Hygiene was a matter of life and death. It was typical of Washington that after one visit to Fisk University, he complained to the president that the outhouses were filthy and that the students had no place to bathe. His concern for cleanliness led him to support Negro Health Week, launched at Tuskegee in 1915, a major effort to reduce mortality in the black community.

Washington criticized but never belittled the black community. Blacks might be ignorant, he argued, but they were not degraded. Far from being indolent, he told whites, "the masses of the colored people work hard, but . . . someone else receives the profits." To those who alleged that blacks had little reverence for family life, Washington pointed out that blacks took care of their dependents to a greater degree, perhaps, than any other race. "In all my experience in the South, I do not think I have ever seen a little child suffering by reason of the fact that no one would take him into his family." While criticizing many black ministers for being ignorant and immoral—valid criticisms—he praised the sincerity and passion of black religious faith. Educated blacks often cringed when Washington put on a thick dialect and told "darky" stories. But Washington understood that blacks, like most groups, were quite able to laugh at themselves if the joke were funny and it came from the right person.

Conciliation

Did Washington concede too much? Did he, by his failure to join the forces of protest, aid and abet the white supremacy movement? Although only two states, Mississippi and South Carolina, had actually disfranchised blacks by 1895, disfranchisement was an unstoppable movement. As for segregation, blacks and whites already lived separate social lives, hardly ever intermarried, worshipped at separate churches, and attended separate schools. Separation was also the custom in saloons, hotels, restaurants, and other public accommodations. These forms of separation, moreover, were by and large accepted by blacks, some more grudgingly than others. The main area of contention was public transportation: blacks bitterly resented being relegated to filthy railway carriages and assigned to the back seats of streetcars. Like disfranchisement, however, the onward march of Jim Crow was irresistible. W.E.B. Du Bois, then a professor at Atlanta University who became Washington's most influential critic, charged that conciliation of the white South had made a bad situation worse. On the other hand, Kelly Miller, who taught at Howard University, argued that "no human power could stay the wave of race hatred now sweeping over the country." There is ample evidence that Washington harbored deep anger about lynching, peonage, convict labor, Jim Crow laws, the neglect of black schools, and what he called the "cancer of discrimination." As historian Donald J. Calista put it, "beneath his ingratiating manner boiled a man filled with contempt for the injustices done to his race by whites." Behind the scenes, Washington fought disfranchisement, challenged railroad segregation, attacked peonage, and opposed the exclusion of blacks from juries.

From Washington's point of view, however, a strategy of open protest—as practiced by Ida B. Wells, for example—would be barren of results and may even, by antagonizing white Southerners, make life even more difficult for blacks in the South. "It takes more courage, in my opinion, for one to keep his mouth closed than to open it," he once explained, "especially when he is a thousand miles from the seat of real danger." Washington knew the precariousness of his own position, and that of Tuskegee Institute. Despite Tuskegee's relative independence, its autonomy was not absolute; the state legislature could wreak serious damage if it chose to do so. And no black person in the South, however well-connected, was beyond reach of white retribution.

The cost of militancy was vividly illustrated by the experiences of two other men who headed black colleges in Alabama. William H. Councill, black president of State Normal and Industrial School in Huntsville, was forced to resign in 1887 after he sued the Atlantic Railroad Company for racial discrimination in evicting him from a first-class carriage. In the same year, in the town of Marion, black students from Colored University fought with white students from Howard College, and black townspeople boycotted white merchants. The Alabama legislature thereupon punished William B. Paterson, the white president of Colored University, by abolishing his school. Councill eventually got his job back, and thereafter accorded Alabama's Democrats unswerving devotion. Paterson succeeded in reestablishing his school in Montgomery, but the legislature denied it the name of "university." These happenings reinforced what Washington already knew: if he forcefully and repeatedly criticized racial discrimination, his position in Alabama would become untenable.

Black Powerlessness

Washington then, was a product of black powerlessness. Black political leadership was headed toward extinction, and Washington stepped into the opening vacuum. He proposed a strategy for dealing with the unenviable situation in which black Southerners found themselves. He tried to find a means whereby blacks could find a secure economic niche in the New South, even if they had to surrender their political rights and some of their civil rights. Despite his conservatism, however, Washington never renounced the ultimate goal of equality. He advocated a tactical retreat in order to prepare the way for a strategic advance.

Yet did the gains secured by Washington justify the refusal to protest, the abandoning of politics, and the apparent endorsement of segregation? Many doubted it. Charles W. Chesnutt complained to Washington that "you Southern educators are all bound up with some special cause or other, devotion to which sometimes warps your judgment as to what is best for the general welfare of the race. Your institution, your system of education . . . is apt to dwarf everything else and become the sole remedy for social and political evils which have a much wider basis." Even staunch ally T. Thomas Fortune felt uneasy about Washington's denigration of politics and lack of vigor in opposing disfranchisement. "It is not necessary to give away the *whole* political case in order to propagate the industrial idea."

Many blacks found Washington's accommodationism deeply humiliating. "If we are not striving for equality, in heaven's name for what are we living?" asked black teacher John Hope in 1896. "If money, education, and honesty will not bring to me as much privilege, as much equality as they bring to any American citizen, then they are to me a curse, and not a blessing." Even if Washington's accomplishments are taken into account, therefore, they need to be balanced by the psychological damage that the policy of appeasing the white South may have inflicted upon both individuals and the race as a whole. As historian Lawrence J. Friedman has suggested, the "material gains may have been dwarfed against the psychic gains he could have rendered blacks had he been openly defiant and patently courageous." Friedman also speculated that his repression of anger and masking of feelings "may have . . . inflicted physical as well as psychological damage" upon Washington himself.

For many black Southerners, however, and for Washington himself, the strategy of accommodation provided self-respect and psychological comfort. Washington was correct in sensing that few people could base their lives upon agitation and protest. Protest meant defining oneself in opposition to whites, and continually dwelling upon the negative effects of discrimination. Nothing was more frustrating and discouraging, moreover, than engaging in protest when circumstances made it barren of results. To Washington, agitation wasted energy that could be better devoted to self-improvement and racial uplift. "If one wants to be made to feel real sick and disconsolate he needs but to share the experience of sitting in an Afro-American meeting and hear two or three Negro speakers speak for two or three hours describing the ills of the Negro race. . . . In some places the race makes no effort to go forward in the direction that other races are working because it has gotten into the habit of crying and can do nothing else." Writing to his daughter Portia, then studying in the North, he warned her not to "dwell too much upon American prejudice, or any other race prejudice. The thing is for one to get above such things." Washington's message of self-help held such a powerful appeal to many black Southerners, especially the middle class, because it coincided with aspirations and beliefs they already held.

Washington believed that he spoke to, and for, the black masses. It was not such a vain delusion: he was the only black leader of his age who could consistently attract large and enthusiastic audiences. Writing in 1937, historian Horace Mann Bond tried to analyze Washington's appeal:

> Those persons who have praised Booker T. Washington most loudly in the past . . . by far underestimate him. To them Booker T. Washington is a sort of mythical figure who preached humility and manual labor for Negroes. To me he is a man who

came to understand the American culture—and that of the South—as no man before or since him could. More, in his life and person he translated that understanding into action, by means of a personality so rare and compelling that he could appeal with equal force, not only to Northern financiers and scholars, but also to the most illiterate Negroes in the lower South.

Not until Martin Luther King, Jr., achieved fame forty years later would another Southern black leader command such influence and popularity.

Viewpoint 5

"Negroes can build a mammoth machine of mass action . . . that can shatter and crush the evil fortress of race prejudice and hate."

Civil Rights Can Be Secured Through Mass Action

A. Philip Randolph

A. Philip Randolph was the preeminent black labor leader of the twentieth century. As president of the Brotherhood of Sleeping Car Porters and later as a key figure in the civil rights movement, Randolph fought throughout his career to bolster economic and political rights for the black working class.

Randolph gained national prominence when World War II exposed a new facet of the nation's longstanding racial problem: Nearly a million African Americans defended their country by serving in the armed forces—where segregated units were a grim reminder of Jim Crow. At the same time, blacks were excluded from all but the most menial defense industry jobs. To compel the federal government to desegregate its defense industries, Randolph called on blacks to march on Washington on July 1, 1941. His address, reprinted here, is taken from an article

A. Philip Randolph, "Call to Negro America to March on Washington for Jobs and Equal Participation in National Defense on July 1, 1941," *The Black Worker*, May 14, 1941.

in the *Black Worker*, the publication of the Brotherhood of Sleeping Car Porters.

Faced with the prospect of thousands of blacks marching on Washington, D.C., President Franklin D. Roosevelt acquiesced to Randolph's demands and issued an executive order that prohibited discrimination in the defense industries. Although the July 1 march was called off, Randolph's ideas on mass action campaigns spawned much of the ideology that would later dominate the civil rights movement.

W e call upon you to fight for jobs in National Defense. We call upon you to struggle for the integration of Negroes in the armed forces, such as the Air Corps, Navy, Army and Marine Corps of the Nation.

We call upon you to demonstrate for the abolition of Jim-Crowism in all Government departments and defense employment.

An Hour of Crisis

This is an hour of crisis. It is a crisis of democracy. It is a crisis of minority groups. It is a crisis of Negro Americans.

What is this crisis?

To American Negroes, it is the denial of jobs in Government defense projects. It is racial discrimination in Government departments. It is widespread Jim-Crowism in the armed forces of the Nation.

While billions of the taxpayers' money are being spent for war weapons, Negro workers are being turned away from the gates of factories, mines and mills—being flatly told, "NOTHING DO-ING." Some employers refuse to give Negroes jobs when they are without "union cards," and some unions refuse Negro workers union cards when they are "without jobs."

What shall we do?

What a dilemma!

What a runaround!

What a disgrace!

What a blow below the belt!

'Though dark, doubtful and discouraging, all is not lost, all is not hopeless. 'Though battered and bruised, we are not beaten, broken or bewildered.

Verily, the Negroes' deepest disappointments and direst defeats, their tragic trials and outrageous oppressions in these dreadful days of destruction and disaster to democracy and freedom, and the rights of minority peoples, and the dignity and independence of the human spirit, is the Negroes' greatest opportunity to rise to the highest heights of struggle for freedom and justice in Government, in industry, in labor unions, education, social service, religion and culture.

Self-Liberation

With faith and confidence of the Negro people in their own power for self-liberation, Negroes can break down the barriers of discrimination against employment in National Defense. Negroes can kill the deadly serpent of race hatred in the Army, Navy, Air and Marine Corps, and smash through and blast the Government, business and labor-union red tape to win the right to equal opportunity in vocational training and re-training in defense employment.

Most important and vital to all, Negroes, by the mobilization and coordination of their mass power, can cause PRESIDENT ROOSEVELT TO ISSUE AN EXECUTIVE ORDER ABOLISHING DISCRIMINATIONS IN ALL GOVERNMENT DEPARTMENTS, ARMY, NAVY, AIR CORPS AND NATIONAL DEFENSE JOBS.

Of course, the task is not easy. In very truth, it is big, tremendous and difficult.

It will cost money.

It will require sacrifice.

It will tax the Negroes' courage, determination and will to struggle. But we can, must and will triumph.

The Negroes' stake in national defense is big. It consists of jobs, thousands of jobs. It may represent millions, yes, hundreds of millions of dollars in wages. It consists of new industrial opportunities and hope. This is worth fighting for.

But to win our stakes, it will require an "all-out," bold and total effort and demonstration of colossal proportions.

Negroes can build a mammoth machine of mass action with a

terrific and tremendous driving and striking power that can shatter and crush the evil fortress of race prejudice and hate, if they will only resolve to do so and never stop, until victory comes. Dear fellow Negro Americans, be not dismayed in these terrible times. You possess power, great power. Our problem is to harness and hitch it up for action on the broadest, daring and most gigantic scale.

Aggressive Mass Action

In this period of power politics, nothing counts but pressure, more pressure, and still more pressure, through the tactic and strategy of broad, organized, aggressive mass action behind the vital and important issues of the Negro. To this end, we propose that ten thousand Negroes MARCH ON WASHINGTON FOR JOBS IN NATIONAL DEFENSE AND EQUAL INTEGRATION IN THE FIGHTING FORCES OF THE UNITED STATES.

An "all-out" thundering march on Washington, ending in a monster and huge demonstration at Lincoln's Monument will shake up white America.

It will shake up official Washington.

It will give encouragement to our white friends to fight all the harder by our side, with us, for our righteous cause.

It will gain respect for the Negro people.

It will create a new sense of self-respect among Negroes.

But what of national unity?

We believe in national unity which recognizes equal opportunity of black and white citizens to jobs in national defense and the armed forces, and in all other institutions and endeavors in America. We condemn all dictatorships, Fascist, Nazi and Communist. We are loyal, patriotic Americans, all.

But, if American democracy will not defend its defenders; if American democracy will not protect its protectors; if American democracy will not give jobs to its toilers because of race or color; if American democracy will not insure equality of opportunity, freedom and justice to its citizens, black and white, it is a hollow mockery and belies the principles for which it is supposed to stand.

To the hard, difficult and trying problem of securing equal participation in national defense, we summon all Negro Americans to march on Washington. We summon Negro Americans to form committees in various cities to recruit and register marchers and raise funds through the sale of buttons and other legitimate means for the expenses of marchers to Washington by buses, train, private automobiles, trucks, and on foot.

We summon Negro Americans to stage marches on their City Halls and Councils in their respective cities and urge them to memorialize the President to issue an executive order to abolish discrimination in the Government and national defense.

However, we sternly counsel against violence and ill-considered and intemperate action and the abuse of power. Mass power, like physical power, when misdirected is more harmful than helpful.

We summon you to mass action that is orderly and lawful, but aggressive and militant, for justice, equality and freedom.

Crispus Attucks marched and died as a martyr for American independence. Nat Turner, Denmark Vesey, Gabriel Prosser, Harriet Tubman and Frederick Douglass fought, bled and died for the emancipation of Negro slaves and the preservation of American democracy.

Abraham Lincoln, in times of the grave emergency of the Civil War, issued the Proclamation of Emancipation for the freedom of Negro slaves and the preservation of American democracy.

Freedom from Stigma

Today, we call upon President Roosevelt, a great humanitarian and idealist, to follow in the footsteps of his noble and illustrious predecessor and take the second decisive step in this world and national emergency and free American Negro citizens of the stigma, humiliation and insult of discrimination and Jim-Crowism in Government departments and national defense.

The Federal Government cannot with clear conscience call upon private industry and labor unions to abolish discrimination based upon race and color as long as it practices discrimination itself against Negro Americans.

Viewpoint 6

"The attack on discrimination by use of legal machinery has only scratched the surface."

Civil Rights Can Be Secured Through Legal Action

Thurgood Marshall

As lead attorney for the NAACP Legal Defense Fund during the pivotal years of the black freedom struggle, Thurgood Marshall remains one of the most well-known figures of the civil rights movement. Marshall's use of legal strategies to eradicate segregation culminated in many precedent-setting cases. In his twenty-three years with the NAACP, Marshall won twenty-nine of the thirty-two cases he argued before the Supreme Court. His most famous case, *Brown v. Board of Education*, declared segregation of public schools illegal. Marshall went on to become the first black justice to sit on the Supreme Court of the United States.

In the following address before a special wartime conference of the NAACP in 1944, Marshall outlines the legal machinery behind the NAACP's campaign to overturn racial segregation and other forms of discrimination. Critical to the success of the legal campaign, Marshall states, is the enforcement of existing civil rights statutes and the creation of new legislation.

Thurgood Marshall, address to the NAACP Wartime Conference, July 13, 1944.

61

The struggle for full citizenship rights can be speeded by enforcement of existing statutory provisions protecting our civil rights. The attack on discrimination by use of legal machinery has only scratched the surface. An understanding of the existing statutes protecting our civil rights is necessary if we are to work toward enforcement of these statutes.

Defining Civil Rights

The titles "civil rights" and "civil liberties" have grown to include large numbers of subjects, some of which are properly included under these titles and others which should not be included. One legal treatise has defined the subject of civil rights as follows: "In its broadest sense, the term civil rights includes those rights which are the outgrowth of civilization, the existence and exercise of which necessarily follow from the rights that repose in the subjects of a country exercising self-government."

The Fourteenth and Fifteenth Amendments to the Constitution are prohibitions against action by the states and state officers violating civil rights. In addition to these provisions of the United States Constitution and a few others, there are several statutes of the United States which also attempt to protect the rights of individual citizens against private persons as well as public officers. Whether these provisions are included under the title of "civil rights" or "civil liberties" or any other subject is more or less unimportant as long as we bear in mind the provisions themselves.

All of the statutes, both federal and state, which protect the individual rights of Americans are important to Negroes as well as other citizens. Many of these provisions, however, are of peculiar significance to Negroes because of the fact that in many instances these statutes are the only protection to which Negroes can look for redress. It should also be pointed out that many officials of both state and federal governments are reluctant to protect the rights of Negroes. It is often difficult to enforce our rights when they are perfectly clear. It is practically impossible to secure enforcement of any of our rights if there is any doubt whatsoever as to whether or not a particular statute applies to the particular state of facts.

As to law enforcement itself, the rule as to most American citizens is that if there is any way possible to prosecute individuals who have willfully interfered with the rights of other individuals such prosecution is attempted. However, when the complaining party is a Negro, the rule is usually to look for any possible grounds for *not* prosecuting. It is therefore imperative that Negroes be thoroughly familiar with the rights guaranteed them by law in order that they may be in a position to insist that all of their fundamental rights as American citizens be protected.

The Thirteenth Amendment to the Constitution, abolishing slavery, the Fourteenth Amendment, prohibiting any action of state officials denying due process or the equal protection of its laws, and the Fifteenth Amendment, prohibiting discrimination by the states in voting are well-known to all of us. In addition to these provisions of the Constitution, there are the so-called Federal "Civil Rights Statutes" which include several Acts of Congress such as the Civil Rights Act and other statutes which have been amended from time to time and are now grouped together in several sections of the United States Code. The original Civil Rights Act was passed in Congress in 1866, but was vetoed by President Andrew Johnson the same year. It was, however, passed over the veto. It was reintroduced and passed in 1870 because there was some doubt as to its constitutionality, having been passed before the Fourteenth Amendment was ratified. The second bill has been construed several times and has been held constitutional by the United States Supreme Court, which in one case stated that "the plain objects of these statutes, as of the Constitution which authorized them, was to place the colored race, in respect to civil rights, upon a level with the whites. They made the rights and responsibilities, civil and criminal, of the two races exactly the same." (Virginia v. Rives, 100 U.S. 313 [1879])

The Thirteenth and Fourteenth and Fifteenth Amendments, along with the civil rights statutes, protect the following rights:

1. Slavery is abolished and peonage is punishable as a federal crime. (13th amendment)

2. All persons born or naturalized in the U.S. are citizens and no state shall make or enforce any law abridging their privileges or immunities, or deny them equal protection of the law. (14th amendment)

3. The right of citizens to vote cannot be abridged by the United

States or by any state on account of race or color. (15th amendment)

4. All persons within the jurisdiction of the United States shall have the same right to enforce contracts, or sue, be parties, give evidence, and to the full and equal benefit of all laws and proceedings as is enjoyed by white citizens.

5. All persons shall be subject to like punishment, pains, penalties, taxes, licenses, and extractions of every kind, and to no other.

6. All citizens shall have the same right in every state and territory, as is enjoyed by white citizens to inherit, purchase, lease, sell, hold and convey property.

7. Every person who, under color of statutes, custom or usage, subjects any citizen of the United States or person within the jurisdiction thereof to the deprivation of any rights, privileges, or immunities secured by the Constitution and laws is liable in an action at law, suit in equity, or other proper proceedings for redress.

8. Citizens possessing all other qualifications may not be disqualified from jury service in federal or state courts on account of race or color; any officer charged with the duty of selection or summoning of jurors who shall exclude citizens for reasons of race or color shall be guilty of a misdemeanor.

9. A conspiracy of two or more persons to deprive any person or class of persons of any rights guaranteed by constitution and laws is punishable as a crime and the conspirators are also liable in damages.

Most of these provisions only protect the citizen against wrongdoing by public officials, although the peonage statutes and one or two others protect against wrongs by private persons.

Despite the purposes of these Acts which the United States Supreme Court insisted in 1879 "made the rights and responsibilities, civil and criminal, of the two races exactly the same," the experience of all of us points to the fact that this purpose has not as yet been accomplished. There are several reasons for this. In the first place, in certain sections of this country, especially in the deep south, judges, prosecutors and members of grand and petit juries, have simply refused to follow the letter or spirit of these provisions. Very often it happens that although the judge and prosecutor are anxious to enforce the laws, members of the jury are reluctant to protect the rights of Negroes. A third reason is that many Negroes themselves for one reason or another hesitate to avail themselves of the protection afforded by the United States Constitution and statutes.

These statutes protecting our civil rights in several instances provide for both criminal and civil redress. Some are criminal only and others are for civil action only. Criminal prosecution for violation of the federal statutes can be obtained only through the United States Department of Justice.

Up through and including the administration of Attorney General Homer S. Cummings, Negroes were unable to persuade the U.S. Department of Justice to enforce any of the civil rights statutes where Negroes were the complaining parties. The NAACP and its staff made repeated requests and in many instances filed detailed statements and briefs requesting prosecution for lynch mobs, persons guilty of peonage and other apparent violations of the federal statutes. It was not until the [1939–1940] administration of Attorney General Frank Murphy that any substantial efforts were made to enforce the civil rights statutes as they apply to Negroes. Attorney General Murphy established a Civil Rights Section in the Department of Justice.

During the present [1944] administration of Attorney General Francis Biddle there have been several instances of prosecution of members of lynch mobs for the first time in the history of the United States Department of Justice. There have also been numerous successful prosecutions of Persons guilty of peonage and slavery. However, other cases involving the question of the beating and killing of Negro soldiers by local police officers, the case involving the action of Sheriff Tip Hunter, of Brownsville, Tennessee, who killed at least one Negro citizen and forced several others to leave town, the several cases of refusal to permit qualified Negroes to vote, as well as other cases, have received the attention of the Department of Justice only to the extent of "investigating." Our civil rights as guaranteed by the federal statutes will never become a reality until the U.S. Department of Justice decides that it represents the entire United States and is not required to fear offending any section of the country which believes that it has the God-given right to be above the laws of the United States and the United States Supreme Court. . . .

There are, however, certain bright spots in the enforcement of the federal statutes. In addition to the lynching and peonage cases handled by the Washington office of the Department of Justice, there have been a few instances of courageous United States Attorneys in such places as Georgia who have vigorously prosecuted police officers who have used the power of their office as a cloak for beating up Negro citizens.

An Example of Civil Rights Enforcement

As a result of the recent decision in the Texas Primary Case [*Smith v. Allwright*], it is possible to use an example of criminal prosecution under the civil rights statutes by taking a typical case of the refusal to permit the Negroes to vote in the Democratic Primary election. Let us see how a prosecution is started: In Waycross, Georgia, for example, we will suppose a Negro elector on July 4, 1944, went to the polls with his tax receipt and demanded to vote in the Democratic Primary. He should, of course, have witnesses with him. Let us also assume that the election officials refused to let him vote solely because of his race or color.

As a matter of law, the election officials violated a federal criminal law and are subject to fine and imprisonment. But how should the voter or the organized Negro citizens, or the local NAACP Branch go about trying to get the machinery of criminal justice in motion? Of course, the details of what happens must be put in writing and sworn to by the person who tried to vote and also by his witnesses. Then the matter must be placed before the United States Attorney. This is the *federal* district attorney.

I wonder how many of the delegates here know who is the United States Attorney for their district, or even where his office is. Every Branch should know the United States Attorney for that area, even if a delegation goes in just to get acquainted and let him know that we expect him to enforce the civil rights laws with the same vigor as used in enforcing other criminal statutes.

But back to the voting case. The affidavits must be presented to the United States Attorney with a demand that he investigate and place the evidence before the Federal Grand Jury. At the same time copies of the affidavits and statements in the case should be sent to the National Office. We will see that they get to the Attorney General in Washington. I wish that I could guarantee you that the Attorney General would put pressure on local United States Attorneys who seem reluctant to prosecute. At least we can assure you that we will give the Attorney General no rest unless he gets behind these reluctant United States attorneys throughout the south.

There is no reason why a hundred clear cases of this sort should not be placed before the United States Attorneys and the Attorney General every year until the election officials discover that it is both wiser and safer to follow the United States laws than to violate them. It is up to us to see that these officials of the Department of Justice are called upon to act again and again wherever there are violations of the civil rights statutes. Unfortunately, there are plenty of such cases. It is equally unfortunate that there are not enough individuals and groups presenting these cases and demanding action.

Neglected Civil Rights Statutes

The responsibility for enforcement of the civil provisions of the civil rights statutes rests solely with the individual. In the past we have neglected to make full use of these statutes. Although they have been on the books since 1870, there were very few cases under these statutes until recent years. Whereas in the field of general law there are many, many precedents for all other types of action, there are very few precedents for the protection of civil liberties.

The most important of the civil rights provisions is the one which provides that "every person who, under color of any statute, ordinance, regulation, custom or usage of any state or territory, subjects or causes to be subjected any citizen of the United States or person within the jurisdiction thereof to the deprivation of any rights, privileges or immunities secured by the Constitution and laws shall be liable to the party injured in an action at law, suit in equity or other proper proceeding for redress." Under this statute any officer of a state, county or municipality who while acting in an official capacity, denies to any citizen or person within the state any of the rights guaranteed by the Constitution or laws is subject to a civil action. This statute has been used to equalize teachers' salaries and to obtain bus transportation for Negro schoolchildren. It can be used to attack *every* form of discrimination against Negroes by public school systems. . . .

This statute, along with other of the civil rights statutes, can be used to enforce the right to register and vote throughout the country. The threats of many of the bigots in the south to disregard the ruling of the Supreme Court of the United States in the recent Texas Primary decision has not intimidated a single person. The United States Supreme Court remains the highest court in this land. Election officials in states affected by this decision will either let Negroes vote in the Democratic Primaries, or they will be subjected to both criminal and civil prosecution under the civil rights statutes. In every state in the deep south Negroes have this year attempted to vote in the primary elections. Affidavits concerning the refusal to permit them to vote in Alabama, Florida and Georgia have already been sent to the United States Department of Justice. We will insist that these election officials be prosecuted and will also file civil suits against the guilty officials.

It can be seen from these examples that we have just begun to scratch the surface in the fight for full enforcement of these statutes. The NAACP can move no faster than the individuals who have been discriminated against. We only take up cases where we are requested to do so by persons who have been discriminated against.

Another crucial problem is the ever-present problem of segregation. Whereas the principle has been established by cases handled by the NAACP that neither states nor municipalities can pass ordinances segregating residences by race, the growing problem today is the problem of segregation by means of restrictive covenants, whereby private owners band together to prevent Negro occupancy of particular neighborhoods. Although this problem is particularly acute in Chicago, it is at the same time growing in intensity throughout the country. It has the full support of the real estate boards in the several cities, as well as most of the banks and other leading agencies. The legal attack on this problem has met with spotty success. In several instances restrictive covenants have been declared invalid because the neighborhood has changed, or for other reasons. Other cases have been lost. However, the NAACP is in the process of preparing a detailed memorandum and will establish procedure which will lead to an all-out legal attack on restrictive covenants. Whether or not this attack will be successful cannot be determined at this time. [Editor's note: In 1948 the Supreme Court in *Shelley v. Kraemer* ruled that racially restrictive covenants could not be legally enforced under the Constitution.]

The National Housing Agency and the Federal Public Housing Authority have established a policy of segregation in federal public housing projects. A test case has been filed in Detroit, Mich., and is still pending in the local federal courts. The Detroit situation is the same as in other sections of the country. Despite the fact that the Housing Authority and other agencies insist that they will maintain separate but equal facilities, it never develops that the separate facilities are equal in all respects. In Detroit separate projects were built and it developed that by the first of this year every single white family in the area eligible for public housing had been accommodated and there were still some 800 "white" units vacant with "no takers." At the same time there were some 45,000 Negroes inadequately housed and with no units open to them. This is the inevitable result of "separate but equal" treatment....

State Laws

We should also be mindful of the several so-called civil rights statutes in the several states. There are civil rights acts in at least 18 states, all of which are in the north and middle west. These statutes are in California, Colorado, Connecticut, Illinois, Indiana, Iowa, Kansas, Massachusetts, Michigan, Minnesota, Nebraska, New Jersey, New York, Ohio, Pennsylvania, Rhode Island and Washington. California provides only for civil action. Illinois, Kansas, Minnesota, New York and Ohio have both civil and criminal provisions. In New Jersey the only action is a criminal action, or an action for penalty in the name of the state, the amount of the penalty going to the state.

In those states not having civil rights statutes it is necessary that every effort be made to secure passage of one. In states having weak civil rights statutes efforts should be made to have them strengthened. In states with reasonably strong civil rights statutes, like Illinois and New York, it is necessary that every effort be made to enforce them....

Outside of New York City there are very few successful cases against the civil rights statutes because of the fact that members of the jury are usually reluctant to enforce the statutes. I understand the same is true for Illinois. The only method of counteracting this vicious practice is by means of educating the general public, from which juries are chosen, to the plight of the Negro.

It should also be pointed out that many of our friends of other races are not as loud and vociferous as the enemies of our race. In northern and mid-western cities it repeatedly happens that a prejudiced southerner on entering a hotel or restaurant, seeing Negroes present makes an immediate and loud protest to the manager. It is very seldom that any of our friends go to the managers of places where Negroes are excluded and complain to them of this fact. Quite a job can be done if our friends of other races will only realize the importance of this problem and get up from their comfortable chairs and actually go to work on the problem.

Bring Civil Rights Violators to Justice

Thus it seems clear that although it is necessary and vital to all of us that we continue our program for additional legislation to guarantee and enforce certain of our rights, at the same time we must continue with ever-increasing vigor to enforce those few statutes, both federal and state, which are now on the statute books. We must not be delayed by people who say "the time is not ripe," nor should we proceed with caution for fear of destroying the "status quo." Persons who deny to us our civil rights should be brought to justice now. Many people believe the time is always "ripe" to discriminate against Negroes. All right then—the time is always "ripe" to bring them to justice. The responsibility for the enforcement of these statutes rests with every American citizen regardless of race or color. However, the real job has to be done by the Negro population with whatever friends of the other races are willing to join in.

CHAPTER 2

Segregation or Integration?

✸ Chapter Preface

Although the civil rights movement sought to dismantle all forms of racial injustice, one of its most pointed goals was the elimination of segregation, the attempt by many white southerners to separate the races in virtually every sphere of life. Segregation gained a legal foothold in the historic case *Plessy v. Ferguson*, which revolved around Homer Plessy, a black shoemaker in Louisiana, who was arrested in 1892 after he boarded a train and took a seat in the whites-only section. In the case that followed, the court ruled that Louisiana had a right to prevent racial mixing. Separating passengers, according to the decision, did not violate the equal protection clause of the Fourteenth Amendment as long as the accommodations for blacks and whites were "substantially equal." The effects of the ruling were profound. *Plessy v. Ferguson* and its "separate but equal" doctrine spawned the Jim Crow laws, a new wave of segregation laws named after a buffoonish black minstrel show character. In the age of Jim Crow, many southern states segregated their restaurants, buses, parks, lavatories, movie theaters, and other public places. Moreover, the separate facilities for blacks and whites were rarely, if ever, equal.

To many, the best chance for eradicating Jim Crow lay in dismantling the legal foundations that upheld the "separate but equal" doctrine. By the 1940s civil rights workers had already made progress in outlawing discrimination in the defense industries and the armed forces. At the same time, lawyers for the National Association for the Advancement of Colored People had presented a series of cases before the Supreme Court arguing that segregation meant inherently unequal facilities. These cases culminated in the Court's 1954 landmark decision *Brown v. Board of Education*, which declared that separate educational facilities were inherently unequal and therefore unconstitutional.

The historic *Brown* ruling seemed to demonstrate that the Court could undermine southern segregation practices. Yet resistance to *Brown* was fierce, especially in the Deep South, where the most ardent segregationists refused to comply on the grounds that the

Court had illegitimately usurped local authority, which rendered the federal ruling invalid. To circumvent desegregation, southern leaders and residents launched a concerted effort that included legal appeals and the formation of White Citizens' Councils, white supremacist groups that used a variety of measures to resist integration and maintain the southern way of life. Some even debated whether blacks desired integration at all.

Opposition to the mandates set forth in *Brown* ultimately ushered in an era of black activism as African Americans and their white allies sought not only to implement *Brown* but also to extend its principles to all areas of public life. The movement that was born in the drive to desegregate—the boycotts, sit-ins, and demonstrations of the 1950s and 1960s—became known as the civil rights movement.

Viewpoint 1

"Racial segregation in our country is immoral, costly, and damaging to the nation's prestige."

Segregation Is Morally Wrong

Thurgood Marshall

Throughout his legal career, Thurgood Marshall used the courts to expose Jim Crow practices and dismantle the legal foundations of segregation. In the 1954 *Brown v. Board of Education,* his most famous case and perhaps one of the most important cases in American history, Marshall pleaded the legal case against segregation in the public schools. On the eve of his decisive victory in the case, Marshall delivered a lecture at Dillard University in New Orleans. In the following speech, which originally appeared in the *Edwin R. Embree Memorial Lectures,* Marshall explains why America's discriminatory racial practices violate the Judeo-Christian ethic and the democratic creed upon which the nation is built, deeming segregation "just as unscientifically supported, immoral, and un-American as slavery."

There has been much discussion during recent years concerning the question of the removal in this country of dual citizenship based solely on race and color. The primary emphasis has been on the elimination of racial segregation. No one denies that progress is

Thurgood Marshall, *The Edwin R. Embree Memorial Lectures.* New Orleans: Dillard University.

being made. There are, however, some who say that the progress is too slow and others who say that the progress is too rapid. The important thing to remember is that progress is being made. We are moving ahead. We have passed the crossroads. We are moving toward a completely integrated society, North and South.

Those who doubt this and those who are afraid of complete integration are victims of a background based upon long indoctrination of only one side of the controversy in this country. They know only of one side of the controversy in this country. They know only of one side of slavery. They know only the biased reports about Reconstruction and the long-standing theory which seems to support the "legality" of the separate-but-equal doctrine.

In order to adequately appraise the situation, we must first understand the problem in relation to our history—legal and political. Secondly, we must give proper weight to progress that has been made with and without legal pressure, and thirdly, we must look to the future.

Our government is based on the principle of the equality of man the individual, not the group. All of us can quote the principle that "All men are created equal." Our basic legal document, the Constitution of the United States, guarantees equal protection of the laws to all of us. Many state constitutions have similar provisions. We even have a "Bill of Rights" in the Constitution of Louisiana. These high-sounding principles we preach and teach. However, in the eyes of the world we stand convicted of violating these principles day in and day out.

Today, one hundred and seventy-seven years after the signing of the Declaration of Independence and eighty-six years after the Fourteenth Amendment was adopted, we have a society where, in varying degrees throughout the country, but especially in the South, Negroes, solely because they are Negroes, are segregated, ostracized and set apart from all other Americans. This discrimination extends from the cradle to the graveyard. (And I emphasize grave*yard*, rather than grave.) Or, to put it even more bluntly, in many areas of this country, a white paroled murderer would be welcome in places which would at the same time exclude such people as Ralph Bunche, Marian Anderson, Jackie Robinson, and many others. Constitutionally protected individual rights have been effectively destroyed by outmoded theories of racial or group inferiority. Why is this true? How long can we afford the luxury of segregation and discrimination?

Historical Background

One reason this condition of dual citizenship exists is because we have been conditioned to an acceptance of this theory as a fact. We are the products of a misunderstanding of history. As a matter of fact, only in recent years have accurate studies of the pre-Civil War period and the Reconstruction period of our history been published.

Our position today is tied up with our past history—at least as far back as the 1820's. At that time the antislavery movement was beginning to take permanent form. It should be borne in mind that those people in New England, Ohio and other areas, who started this movement became dedicated to a principle which has become known as the Judaeo-Christian ethic. This principle was carried forth in their determination to remove slavery from our society, and to remove the badges of caste and inferiority whereby an American could be ostracized or set apart from fellow Americans solely because of race. Of course, slavery per se was the immediate objective—the abolition of slavery—but the ultimate goal was the same as the unfinished business we have before us today, namely, to remove race and caste from the American life.

These people in the 1820 period—1820 to 1865—sought to translate their moral theories and principles into law. They started by pamphleteering and speechmaking. They recognized that equal protection of the laws must always be, in part, an ethical and moral concept, rather than a law. They sought to constitutionalize this moral argument or ideal. Slavery—with its theories of racial damnation, racial inferiority and racial discrimination— was inherently repugnant to the American creed and Christian ethics. They sought to support their moral theories by use of the Declaration of Independence and certain sections of the Constitution as it existed at that time. In so far as public meetings were concerned, speakers were barred from such meetings in the South—brutally beaten or killed, and many were run out of similar meetings in Northern cities and towns. It was, therefore, impossible to get behind the original iron curtain to get public support for much of the program.

In their legal attack they were thwarted by the decision of the United States Supreme Court in the Dred Scott case, which held that no person of African descent, slave or free, had any rights that a white man was bound to respect. The important thing to remember throughout this period is that the opponents of slavery were seeking a Constitutional basis—a legal platform—for the democratic principle of the equality of man.

After the Emancipation Proclamation was signed, many states passed Black Codes and other infamous statutes, effectively returning the emancipated slaves to their inferior status. Consequently, the same people who fought to abolish slavery had to take the lead in Congress in writing the thirteenth, fourteenth and fifteenth amendments.

This short period of intense legislation was followed by the Reconstruction period. Much of that which we have read concerning this period has emphasized, overstated and exaggerated the errors of judgment made in trying to work out the "Negro problem" in such fashion as to give real meaning to these Civil War amendments [but these amendments] were actually thwarted by the conspiracy between Northern capitalists and others to bring "harmony" by leaving the Negro and his problem to the tender mercies of the South. This brought about the separate-but-equal pattern, which spread not only throughout the South but extended and now exists in many Northern and Western areas.

The Equality of Man

Despite the distortion of this historical background, which has become firmly embedded in our minds, is the "understanding" that racial segregation is legal and valid even if in violation of our moral principles. The fallacy of this reasoning is that the equal protection of the laws was intended to be the constitutionalization of the ethic and moral principle of the absolute equality of man—the right of an individual neither to be circumscribed or conditioned by group, race or color.

It should, therefore, be remembered that our society is the victim of the following periods of history: the period of slavery, when the slaveholders defended slavery by repeating over and over again the myth that slavery was not only a positive good for the nation but was absolutely beneficial and necessary for the Negroes themselves. Consequently, even free Negroes were denied the right of citizenship and subjected to all manner of abuse without legal redress. Immediately following the Civil War, and indeed up to the 1930's, is the period when Negroes were no longer slaves but were certainly not yet full citizens. Having passed through this laissez-faire period in so far as asserting our Constitutional rights is concerned, Negroes began in the thirties the all-out fight to secure the right to vote and at the same time to break down discrimination and segregation.

In so far as securing the right to vote, beginning with the registration cases and the white-primary cases and others, much progress has been made to the end that as of the 1948 national elections, at least 1,300,000 Negroes voted in the deep South. We have seen Negroes elected to the city council in Richmond, Virginia, Nashville, Tennessee, and many cities in North Carolina. We have seen Negroes elected to the governing board of the Democratic party in Atlanta, Georgia. We have also seen Negroes elected to school boards in cities such as Atlanta, Georgia, Lynchburg, Virginia, and Winston-Salem, North Carolina. There are still, however, several small areas in Alabama, Mississippi, and at least four parishes in Louisiana where Negroes are still prevented from registering as qualified voters. (But these are distinctly local problems, which are being attended to and can be pushed aside on that basis.)

In the North we have seen the drive for protection of the right to work without regard to race and color—the drive for F.E.P.C. [Fair Employment Practices Committee] legislation. We have seen such legislation passed in at least eight states in the North, leaving forty states and the District of Columbia to go, before we have the necessary safeguards to protect man's right not to be deprived of an opportunity to earn a livelihood because of race, religion or ancestry.

We have also seen the breaking-down of the legal barriers to owning and occupying real property without regard to race or color. Today, as a result of several Supreme Court decisions, any American any place in the United States, regardless of race or color, may own and occupy property wherever he can find a willing seller, has the money to purchase the property and courage to live on it. We still, however, have residential segregation throughout the country, not by law, not by the courts, but by a combination of circumstances, such as, the reactionary policies of mortgage companies and real-estate boards, public-housing agencies, including F.H.A., and other governmental agencies. We also find an unwillingness on the part of many Negroes to exercise their rights in this field. In recent years instead of progress toward an integrated community, we find that the Negro ghetto is merely expanding into a larger and more glorified and gilded ghetto. This unwillingness to exercise our own rights is due in part to the long indoctrination that we are different from or inferior to others and therefore should voluntarily segregate ourselves.

America's Racial Practices

As of the present time, the paramount issue in so far as Americanism is concerned is the ending of all racial distinctions in American life. The reasons for this are many. A weighty factor, of course, is the recognition by more and more people in high places that the world situation in regard to the sensitive areas throughout the world depends on how well we can handle our race problem in this country. Our country can no longer tolerate an Achilles heel of discriminatory practices toward its darker citizens. Even more important is the realization that the equality of man as a principle and the equal protection of the laws as a Constitutional concept are both based upon the moral principle of individual responsibility rather than racial identity.

Racial segregation in our country is immoral, costly, and damaging to the nation's prestige. Segregation and discrimination violate the Judaeo-Christian ethic, and the democratic creed on which our national morality is based is soundly established in the minds of most men. But in addition, it has been shown that the costs of segregation and discrimination to the nation are staggering. Elmo Roper, social scientist and pollster of American public opinion, has stated, "The resultant total of the cost of discrimination comes to roughly $10 out of every $75 paycheck, or, in total, $30 billion lost every year." This figure alone would amount

Three African American women protest segregation. Before the civil rights movement, Jim Crow laws prohibited the integration of public schools.

to a cost of $2,000 per year to every individual in America. But perhaps even more damaging to the nation is the current effect of America's racial practices on America's role in international affairs and world leadership. According to a recent statement by our State Department experts, nearly half of the recent Russian propaganda about America has been concentrated on race, linking Communist germ-warfare charges with alleged racial brutality in this country. In addition, Americans returning from abroad consistently report having been questioned over and over about racial problems in this country.

This concern about American racial practices seems especially strong among the two thirds of the world that is darker-skinned. Our former ambassador to India, Chester Bowles, wrote the following statement, after attending an Indian press conference: "As I later discovered is almost invariably the case in any Asian press conference or forum, the Number One question was, 'What about America's treatment of the Negro?'"

Shortly after returning from a tour of Asian and Pacific areas, Vice-President Nixon made this statement:

> Americans must create a better understanding of American ideals abroad by practicing and thinking tolerance and respect for human rights every day of the year. Every act of racial discrimination or prejudice in the United States hurts Americans as much as an espionage agent who turns over a weapon to a foreign enemy.

Historically, we have to ask whether or not, even as we stand today, our country can afford to continue in practicing *not* what they preach. Historically, the segregation patterns in the United States are carry-overs from the principles of slavery. They are based on the exploded theory of the inferiority of the minority group. Segregation is recognized as resulting from the decision of the majority group without even consulting, less known in seeking, the consent of the segregated group. All of us know that segregation traditionally results in unequal facilities for the segregated group. Duplication of facilities is expensive, diverts funds from the economy which could be utilized to improve facilities for all groups. Finally, segregation leads to the blockage of real communication between the two groups. In turn, this blockage increases mutual suspicion, distrust, hostility, stereotypes and prejudice; and these, all together, result in a social climate of tension favorable to aggressive behavior and social disorganization which sometimes culminate in race riots. Even where we do not have race riots, the seeds of tension are ever present in a segregated system.

Psychological Damage

The harm done to the individual begins with the child's earliest years, when he becomes aware of status differences among groups in society and begins to react to patterns of segregation. Prejudice and discrimination are potentially damaging to the personalities of all children. The children of the majority group are affected differently from those of the minority group. This potential psychological damage is crystallized by segregation practices sanctioned by public law—and it is the same whether in the North, the East, the West, or the South. Damage to the immediate community is inevitable. This is followed by damage to the state, our federal government and, finally, the world today. The only answer is the complete removal of all racial distinctions that lay at the basis of all this.

And now for the future. Everyone in and out of government must understand that the future of our government and indeed the world depends on the recognition of the equality of man—the principle which is inherent in the theory of our government and protected by our Constitution.

Of course, we have made progress, but instead of gloating over this progress, we should get renewed courage to tackle the next job. Let us not listen to the rantings of politicians like Governors [James] Byrnes and Talmadge. Governor Byrnes has declared:

> Should the Supreme Court decide this case against our position, we will face a serious problem. Of only one thing can we be certain. South Carolina will not now, nor for some years to come, mix white and colored children in our schools . . . If the Court changes what is now the law of the land, we will, if it is possible, live within the law, preserve the public-school system, and at the same time maintain segregation. If that is not possible, reluctantly we will abandon the public-school system.

That statement is made by a governor who was formerly a member of the Supreme Court which he is now talking about. Governor Herman Talmadge announces that if the decision comes down opposed to what he thinks it should be, that *he*, Governor Talmadge, will get together as much of his militia as he can find and challenge the whole United States Army.

Instead of listening to people like this, why not listen to people who speak for the South like Ralph McGill of the Atlanta *Constitution* who writes:

> An end to segregation—when it comes—will not, of course, force people to associate socially. That will remain, as now, personal choice. But it will bring on change—and this is what state legislatures in South Carolina, Georgia, Mississippi, Virginia and Alabama are, or will be, considering. They consider

not how to retain legal segregation—which they see soon ending—but how to effect it without legal compulsion . . . Segregation is on the way out and he who tries to tell the people otherwise does them great disservice. The problem of the future is how to live with the change.

There are still those who will continue to tell us that law is one thing and ethics another. However, I prefer to follow what one legal historian has stated—"Laws and ethics, some men bluntly tell us are separate fields. So indeed they are. But spare America the day when both together do not determine the meaning of equal protection of the laws."

We must understand the slavery background of segregation and we must understand the complete lack of any scientific support for racial superiority or inferiority. We must understand that racial segregation is violative of every religious principle, as I said before. We must never forget what racial segregation did to our parents and is doing to us, and how it will affect our children. We must turn from misunderstanding and fear to intelligent planning, courage and determination.

Individual Reactions

Psychologists acknowledge that to achieve a well-balanced, well-adjusted personality, all human beings require a sense of personal dignity and worth, acknowledged not only within themselves but by the society in which they live—the total society. Not every child reacts to personality conflict in the same way. Behavior patterns depend on such interrelated factors as family relations, social and economic class, general personality patterns and other factors. In the final analysis, however, each segregated child is forced to adjust to conflicts not faced by members of the majority group.

Studies published in the *Journal of Social Psychology* indicate that members of the lower economic class may react to racial frustrations by overaggressive behavior, hostility toward the minority group and/or the majority group, and by antisocial behavior. These reactions are self-destructive inasmuch as society not only punishes the offenders but often interprets such behavior as justification for continuing segregation practices against all members of the group. These studies further indicate that members of the middle upper class may react by withdrawal, submissive behavior or rigid conformity to the expected pattern of segregation. Psychologically, this is equally bad.

Generally, however, children of all classes react by adopting an over-all defeatist attitude, a lowering of personal ambitions, hypersensitivity and anxiety about relations in a larger society, and a tendency to see hostility or rejection even where it might not exist. This may result in the development and perpetuation of generally sensitive, conflicting personalities.

Although the range of individual reaction in terms of behavior and personality patterns is very wide, there is no question that all minority children are necessarily affected adversely by enforced segregation—and there is not a single scientific study to the contrary.

While the effects of enforced segregation on majority-group children are more obscure, they are, nevertheless, real. Children who are taught prejudice, directly or indirectly, are also taught to gain and evaluate themselves on a totally unrealistic basis. Perceiving minority-group members as inferior does not permit a member of the majority group to evaluate himself in terms of actual ability or achievement but permits and encourages self-deception—that is, "I am at least better than a Negro."

A culture which permits and encourages enforced segregation motivates feelings of guilt and necessitates an adjustment to protect against recognizing the injustice of racial fears and hatreds.

The contradiction between moral, religious, democratic principles of the brotherhood of man, the importance of justice or fair play and the actuality of the prejudiced, discriminatory practices of individuals and institutions inevitably results in confusion, conflict, moral cynicism and guilt feelings in the majority group. This conflict, supported by pressure to conform to existing patterns, may result in disrespect for authority, unwholesomeness of ideals of all authorities (parents, political leaders) and a determination to run roughshod over everyone not in the conforming group. Some persons may attempt to resolve this conflict by intensifying hostility toward the minority group or to express self-hatred in aggressive behavior.

Of the large number of social scientists who replied to a questionnaire concerning the probable effect of enforced segregation under conditions of equal facilities, ninety percent replied that, regardless of the equality of the facilities provided, enforced segregation is psychologically harmful to the *minority* group members; eighty percent stated it was their opinion that enforced segregation would have damaging effects also on the *majority*-group members.

Enforced segregation appears to have the same general and psychological effect regardless of the quality of facilities available. (That is to answer any of you who believe that the building of a new Jim Crow high school will solve the problem.) Enforced-segregation public schools offer official recognition, sanction and perpetuation to the assumption of inferiority, a myth which has already been exploded. . . .

The Myth of Racial Superiority

In conclusion, racial segregation is grounded upon the myth of inherent racial superiority. This myth has been completely exploded by all scientific studies. It now stands exposed as a theory which can only be explained as a vehicle for perpetuating racial prejudice. History reveals that racial segregation is a badge of slavery, is just as unscientifically supported, immoral and un-American as slavery. Recent history shows that it can be removed, and that it can be done effectively when approached intelligently.

There is no longer any justification for segregation. There is no longer any excuse for if. There is no longer any reason under the sun why intelligent people should continue to find excuses for not ending segregation in their own community, in the South as well as in the North.

Viewpoint 2

"The Negro race, as a race, plainly is not equal to the white race."

Segregation Is Necessary

James Jackson Kilpatrick

With its momentous 1954 ruling against school segregation in *Brown v. Board of Education*, the Supreme Court had seemingly paved the way for civil rights. Indeed, many border states— Kentucky, Maryland, and Missouri, for example—immediately followed court orders and opened their doors to black students. Farther south, however, Jim Crow remained rampant. Many schools refused to comply, and enforcement of the ruling proved difficult.

James Jackson Kilpatrick, then editor of a Virginia newspaper, was one of the more vocal critics of the *Brown* case—and desegregation in general. In the following selection, excerpted from his 1962 book *The Southern Case for School Integration*, Kilpatrick argues that segregation is necessary and that racial equality is a fallacy. Recounting his southern upbringing, Kilpatrick concludes that—despite their dual citizenship—blacks and whites can and do live in relative harmony.

James Jackson Kilpatrick, "The Evidence," *The Southern Case for School Segregation*. New York: Crowell-Collier, 1962.

The South, in general, feels, no sharp sense of sin at its "treatment of the Negro." The guilt hypothesis is vastly overdrawn. If wrong has been done (and doubtless wrong has been done), we reflect that within the human relationship wrong always has been done, by one people upon another, since tribal cavemen quarreled with club and stone. And whatever the wrongs may have been, the white South emphatically refuses to accept all the wrongs as her own. For the South itself has been wronged—cruelly and maliciously wronged, by men in high places whose hypocrisy is exceeded only by their ignorance, men whose trade is to damn the bigotry of the segregated South by day and to sleep in lily-white Westchester County by night. We are keenly aware, as Perry Morgan remarked in a telling phrase, of a North that wishes to denounce discrimination and have it too.

But let us begin gently. The Southerner who would grope seriously for understanding of his own perplexing region, and the non-Southerner who would seek in earnest to learn more than his textbooks would tell him, cannot make a start with *Brown v. Board of Education* on a May afternoon in 1954. Neither can he begin with *Plessy v. Ferguson* in 1896, or with ratification of the Fourteenth Amendment in 1868, or with Appomattox three years earlier. A start has to be made much earlier, in 1619, when the first twenty Negroes arrived from Africa aboard a Dutch slaver and fastened upon the South a wretched incubus that the belated penances of New Englanders have not expiated at all.

The Dual Society

We of the South have been reared from that day in a strange society that only now—and how uncomfortably!—is becoming known at first hand outside the South. This is the dual society, made up of white and Negro coexisting in an oddly intimate remoteness. It is a way of life that has to be experienced. Children mask their eyes and play at being blind. Even so, some of my Northern friends mask their eyes and play at being Southern; they try to imagine what it must be like to be white in the South, to be Negro in the South. Novelist John Griffin dyed his skin and spent three weeks or so pretending to be Negro, looking for incidents to confirm his prejudices. But a child always knows that he can take his hands from his eyes, and see, that he is not really blind; and those who have not grown up from childhood, and fashioned their whole world from a delicately bounded half a world, cannot comprehend what this is all about. They wash the dye from their imaginations, and put aside *The New York Times*, and awake to a well-ordered society in which the Negroes of their personal acquaintance are sipping martinis and talking of Middle Eastern diplomacy. They form an image of "the Negro" (as men form an image of the French, or the British, or the Japanese) in terms of the slim and elegant Harvard student, the eloquent spokesman of a civil rights group, the trim stenographer in a publishing office: Thurgood Marshall on the bench, Ralph Bunche in the lecture hall. It is a splendid image, finely engraved on brittle glass, an object of universal admiration on the mantle of the *New Republic*. It is an image scarcely known in the South.

My father came from New Orleans. His father, a captain in the Confederate Army, returned from the War and established a prosperous business in ship chandlery there. And though I myself was born in Oklahoma, Father having moved there just prior to World War I, we children visited along the Delta in our nonage. We sailed on Pontchartrain, and crabbed at Pass Christian, and once or twice were taken from school in February to sit spellbound on Canal Street and watch the Mardi Gras go by. Our life in Oklahoma was New Orleans once removed; it was a life our playmates accepted as matter-of-factly as children of a coast accept the tides: The Negroes *were;* we *were.* They had their lives; we had ours. There were certain things one did: A proper white child obeyed the family Negroes, ate with them, bothered them, teased them, loved them, lived with them, learned from them. And there were certain things one did not do: One did not intrude upon their lives, or ask about Negro institutions, or bring a Negro child in the front door. And at five, or six, or seven, one accepted, without question, that Calline and Cubboo, who were vaguely the charges of a Negro gardener up the street, had their schools; and we had ours.

Subconsciousness of Race

Does all this have the air of a chapter from William Gilmore Simms or a post-bellum romance by Thomas Nelson Page? I myself lived it, forty years ago; my own sons have lived it in this generation. My father lived it, and his father before him. For three hundred years, the South has lived with this subconsciousness of race. Who hears a clock tick, or the surf murmur, or the trains pass? Not those who live by the clock or the sea or the track. In the South, the acceptance of racial separation begins in the cradle. What rational man imagines this concept can be shattered overnight?

We had two Negroes who served my family more than twenty years. One was Lizzie. The other was Nash. Lizzie was short and plump and placid, and chocolate-brown; she "lived on," in a room and bath over the garage, and her broad face never altered in its kindness. Nash was short and slim, older, better educated, more a leader; she was African-black; and as a laundress, she came in after church on Sundays, put the clothes down to soak in the basement tubs, gossiped with Lizzie, scolded her, raised Lizzie's sights. On Monday, the two of them did the wash, hanging the clothes on heavy wire lines outside the kitchen door, and late in the afternoon Nash ironed. She pushed the iron with an economical push-push, thump; turn the shirt; push-push, thump. And I would come home from school to the smell of starch and the faint scorch of the iron and the push-push, thump, and would descend to the basement only to be ordered upstairs to wash my hands and change out of school clothes.

Toward the end of their lives, disaster came to both of them. Lizzie went slowly blind, through some affliction no surgeon could correct, and Nash lost the middle three fingers of one hand when her scarf tangled in the bellows of a church organ. Nevertheless, they stayed with us until age at last put them on the sidelines. And as far as love and devotion and respect can reach, they were members of the family. Yet I often have wondered, in later years, did we children know them? Did Mother and Father know them? I do not think we did.

This relationship, loving but unknowing, has characterized the lives of thousands of Southern children on farms and in the cities too. White infants learn to feel invisible fences as they crawl, to sense unwritten boundaries as they walk. And I know this much, that Negro children are brought up to sense these boundaries too. What is so often misunderstood, outside the South, is this delicate intimacy of human beings whose lives are so intricately bound together. I have met Northerners who believe, in all apparent seriousness, that segregation in the South means literally that: *segregation*, the races stiffly apart, never touching. A wayfaring stranger from the New York *Herald Tribune* implied as much in a piece he wrote from Virginia after the school decision. His notion was that whites and Negroes did not even say "good morning" to each other. God in heaven!

A Close Relationship

In plain fact, the relationship between white and Negro in the segregated South, in the country and in the city, has been far closer, more honest, less constrained, than such relations generally have been in the integrated North. In Charleston and New Orleans, among many other cities, residential segregation does not exist, for example, as it exists in Detroit or Chicago. In the country, whites and Negroes are farm neighbors. They share the same calamities—the mud, the hail, the weevils—and they minister, in their own unfelt, unspoken way, to one another. Is the relationship that of master and servant, superior and inferior? Down deep, doubtless it is, but I often wonder if this is more of a wrong to the Negro than the affected, hearty "equality" encountered in the North. In the years I lived on a farm, I fished often with a Negro tenant, hour after hour, he paddling, I paddling, sharing the catch, and we tied up the boat and casually went our separate ways. Before *Brown v. Board of Education*, it never occurred to me that in these peaceful hours I was inflicting upon him wounds of the psyche not likely ever to be undone. I do not believe it occurred to Robert either. This is not the way one goes fly-casting on a millpond, with Gunnar Myrdal invisibly present on the middle thwart. We fish no more. He has been busy in recent years, and I too; and when I came across the flyrod recently, I found the line rotted and the ferrules broken.

I say this relationship "has been," and in the past perfect lies a melancholy change that disturbs many Southerners deeply. In my observation, a tendency grows in much of the white South to acknowledge and to abandon, with no more than a ritual protest, many of the patent absurdities of "Jim Crow." Many of these practices, so deeply resented in recent years by the Negro, may have had some rational basis when they were instituted in the post-Reconstruction period. When the first trolleys came along, the few Negroes who rode them were mostly servants; others carried with them the fragrance of farm or livery stable. A Jim Crow section perhaps made sense in those days. But in my own nonage, during the 1920s, and in the years since then, few Southerners ever paused to examine the reasons for segregation on streetcars. We simply moved the little portable sign that separated white from Negro as a car filled up, and whites sat in front of the sign and Negroes sat behind it. This was the way we rode streetcars. After *Brown v. Board of Education*, when the abiding subconsciousness of the Negro turned overnight into an acute and immediate awareness of the Negro, some of these laws and customs ceased to be subject to reason anyhow; they became, confusingly, matters of strategy; they became occupied ground in an undeclared war, not to be yielded lest their yielding be regarded as needless surrender. Many aspects of our lives have gone that way since. The unwritten rules of generations are now being, in truth, unwritten; in their place, it is proposed by the apostles of instant integration that there be no rules at all. It seems so easy: "What difference does the color of a man's skin make?" "Why not just treat them as equals?" "There is no such thing as race."

Ah, but it is not so easy. The ingrained attitudes of a lifetime cannot be jerked out like a pair of infected molars, and new porcelain dentures put in their place. For this is what our Northern friends will not comprehend: The South, agreeable as it may be to confessing some of its sins and to bewailing its more manifest wickednesses, simply does not concede that at bottom its basic attitude is "infected" or wrong. On the contrary, the Southerner rebelliously clings to what seems to him the hard core of truth in this whole controversy: *Here and now*, in his own communities, in the mid-1960s, the Negro race, as a race, plainly is not equal to the white race, as a race; nor, for that matter, in the wider world beyond, by the accepted judgment of ten thousand years, has the Negro race, as a race, *ever* been the cultural or intellectual equal of the white race, as a race.

This we take to be a plain statement of fact, and if we are not amazed that our Northern antagonists do not accept it as such, we are resentful that they will not even look at the proposition, or hear of it, or inquire into it. Those of us who have ventured to discuss the issues outside the South have discovered, whenever the point arises, that no one is so intolerant of truth as academicians whose profession it is to pursue it. The whole question of race has become a closed question: the earth is a cube, and there's an end to it; Two and two are four, the sun rises in the east, and no race is inferior to any other race. Even the possibility of a conflicting hypothesis is beyond the realm of sober examination. John Hope Franklin, chairman of the history department at Brooklyn College, sees Southern attitudes on race as a "hoax." Their wrongness is "indisputable." To Ashley Montagu, race is a myth. A UNESCO pamphlet makes the flat, unqualified statement that "modern biological and psychological studies of the differences between races do not support the idea that one is superior to another as far as innate potentialities are concerned." And when one inquires, why, pray, has it taken so long for the Negro's innately equal potentialities to emerge, the answers trail off into lamentations on the conditions under which the Negro has lived. Thus, the doctrine of environment, like the principle of charity, is trotted out to conceal a multitude of sins. The fault, if there be any fault, is held to be not in men's genes, but in their substandard housing.

All this is to anticipate some of the points this brief is intended to develop, but it is perhaps as well to know where the argument is going. The South does not wish to be cruel, or unkind, or intolerant, or bigoted; but in this area it does not wish to be unrealistic either. We do not agree that our "prejudice" in this regard is prejudice at all, in the pejorative sense in which the word is widely used. The man who wakes up ten times with a hangover, having had too much brandy the night before, is not "prejudiced" against brandy if on the eleventh occasion he passes the brandy by; he has merely learned to respect its qualities. And what others see as the dark night of our bigotry is regarded, in our own observation, as the revealing light of experience. It guides our feet. As Patrick Henry said, we know no other light to go by.

Viewpoint 3

"We conclude that in the field of public education the doctrine of 'separate but equal' has no place."

School Segregation Is Unconstitutional

Earl Warren

In the 1950s, segregation in the classroom was widely accepted—and even mandated by law in many southern states. On May 17, 1954, the Supreme Court unanimously declared in *Brown v. Board of Education* that separate educational facilities were "inherently unequal." By eradicating one of the legal pillars of segregation, this landmark ruling not only marked the end of the "separate but equal" precedent set forth by the Supreme Court in the 1896 case of *Plessy v. Ferguson*, it also served as a catalyst for expanded black rights during the peak years of the civil rights movement.

The decision of the Court was delivered by Chief Justice Earl Warren, a Republican California governor who had been appointed to the Supreme Court in 1953 by President Dwight Eisenhower. In the following excerpt from the decision, Warren stresses both the importance of education and the detrimental effects of school segregation.

Earl Warren, decision, *Brown v. Board of Education*, 347, U.S. 483, May 17, 1954.

These cases come to us from the States of Kansas, South Carolina, Virginia, and Delaware. They are premised on different facts and different local conditions, but a common legal question justifies their consideration together in this consolidated opinion. In each of the cases, minors of the Negro race, through their legal representatives, seek the aid of the courts in obtaining admission to the public schools of their community on a nonsegregated basis. In each instance, they had been denied admission to schools attended by white children under laws requiring or permitting segregation according to race. This segregation was alleged to deprive the plaintiffs of the equal protection of the laws under the Fourteenth Amendment. In each of the cases other than the Delaware case, a three-judge federal district court denied relief to the plaintiffs on the so-called "separate but equal" doctrine announced by this Court in *Plessy v. Ferguson*. . . . Under that doctrine, equality of treatment is accorded when the races are provided substantially equal facilities, even though these facilities be separate. In the Delaware case, the Supreme Court of Delaware adhered to that doctrine, but ordered that the plaintiffs be admitted to the white schools because of their superiority to the Negro schools.

The plaintiffs contend that segregated public schools are not "equal" and cannot be made "equal," and that hence they are deprived of the equal protection of the laws. Because of the obvious importance of the question presented, the Court took jurisdiction. Argument was heard in the 1952 Term, and reargument was heard this Term on certain questions propounded by the Court.

The Fourteenth Amendment

Reargument was largely devoted to the circumstances surrounding the adoption of the Fourteenth Amendment in 1868. It covered exhaustively consideration of the Amendment in Congress, ratification by the states, then existing practices in racial segregation, and the views of proponents and opponents of the Amendment. This discussion and our own investigation convince us that, although these sources cast some light, it is not enough to resolve the problem with which we are faced. At best, they are inconclusive. The most avid proponents of the post-War Amendments undoubtedly intended them to remove all legal distinctions among "all persons born or naturalized in the United States." Their opponents, just as certainly, were antagonistic to both the letter and the spirit of the Amendments and wished them to have the most limited effect. What others in Congress and the state legislatures had in mind cannot be determined with any degree of certainty.

An additional reason for the inconclusive nature of the Amendment's history, with respect to segregated schools, is the status of public education at that time. In the South, the movement toward free common schools, supported by general taxation, had not yet taken hold. Education of white children was largely in the hands of private groups. Education of Negroes was almost nonexistent, and practically all of the race were illiterate. In fact, any education of Negroes was forbidden by law in some states. Today, in contrast, many Negroes have achieved outstanding success in the arts and sciences as well as in the business and professional world. It is true that public school education at the time of the Amendment had advanced further in the North, but the effect of the Amendment on Northern States was generally ignored in the congressional debates. Even in the North, the conditions of public education did not approximate those existing today. The curriculum was usually rudimentary; ungraded schools were common in rural areas; the school term was but three months a year in many states; and compulsory school attendance was virtually unknown. As a consequence, it is not surprising that there should be so little in the history of the Fourteenth Amendment relating to its intended effect on public education.

In the first cases in this Court construing the Fourteenth Amendment, decided shortly after its adoption, the Court interpreted it as proscribing all state-imposed discriminations against the Negro race. The doctrine of "separate but equal" did not make its appearance in this Court until 1896 in the case of *Plessy v. Ferguson*, . . . involving not education but transportation. American courts have since labored with the doctrines for over half a century. In this Court, there have been six cases involving the "separate but equal" doctrine in the field of public education. In *Cumming v. County Board of Education* . . . and *Gong Lum v. Rice*, . . . the validity of the doctrine itself was not challenged. In more recent cases, all on the graduate school level, inequality was found in that specific benefits enjoyed by white students were denied to Negro students of the same educational qualifications. . . . In none of these cases was it necessary to re-examine the doctrine to grant relief to the Negro plaintiff. And in *Sweatt v. Painter,* . . . the Court expressly reserved decision on the question whether *Plessy v. Ferguson* should be held inapplicable to public education.

In the instant cases, that question is directly presented. Here, unlike *Sweatt v. Painter,* there are findings below that the Negro and white schools involved have been equalized, or are being equalized, with respect to buildings, curricula, qualifications and salaries of teachers, and other "tangible" factors. Our decision, therefore, cannot turn on merely a comparison of these tangible factors in the Negro and white schools involved in each of the cases. We must look instead to the effect of segregation itself on public education.

Segregation and Education

In approaching this problem, we cannot turn the clock back to 1868 when the Amendment was adopted, or even to 1896 when *Plessy v. Ferguson* was written. We must consider public education in the light of its full development and its present place in American life throughout the Nation. Only in this way can it be determined if segregation in public schools deprives these plaintiffs of the equal protection of the laws.

Today, education is perhaps the most important function of state and local governments. Compulsory school attendance laws and the great expenditures for education both demonstrate our recognition of the importance of education to our democratic society. It is required in the performance of our most basic public responsibilities, even service in the armed forces. It is the very foundation of good citizenship. Today it is a principal instrument in awakening the child to cultural values, in preparing him for later professional training, and in helping him to adjust normally to his environment. In these days, it is doubtful that any child may reasonably be expected to succeed in life if he is denied the opportunity of an education. Such an opportunity, where the state has undertaken to provide it, is a right which must be made available to all on equal terms.

We come then to the question presented: Does segregation of children in public schools solely on the basis of race, even though the physical facilities and other "tangible" factors may be equal, deprive the children of the minority group of equal educational opportunities? We believe that it does.

In *Sweatt v. Painter*, . . . in finding that a segregated law school for Negroes could not provide them equal educational opportunities, this Court relied in large part on "those qualities which are incapable of objective measurement but which make for greatness in a law school." In *McLaurin v. Oklahoma State Regents*, . . . the Court, in requiring that a Negro admitted to a white graduate school be treated like all other students, again resorted to intangible considerations: ". . . his ability to study, to engage in discussions and exchange views with other students, and, in general, to learn his profession." Such considerations apply with added force to children in grade and high schools. To separate them from others of similar age and qualifications solely because of their race generates a feeling of inferiority as to their status in the community that may affect their hearts and minds in a way unlikely ever to be undone. The effect of this separation on their educational opportunities was well stated by a finding in the Kansas case by a court which nevertheless felt compelled to rule against the Negro plaintiffs:

> Segregation of white and colored children in public schools has a detrimental effect upon the colored children. The impact is greater when it has the sanction of the law; for the policy of separating the races is usually interpreted as denoting the inferiority of the negro group. A sense of inferiority affects the motivation of a child to learn. Segregation with the sanction of law, therefore, has a tendency to [retard] the education and mental development of negro children and to deprive them of some of the benefits they would receive in a racial[ly] integrated school system.

Whatever may have been the extent of psychological knowledge at the time of *Plessy v. Ferguson*, this finding is amply supported by modern authority. Any language in *Plessy v. Ferguson* contrary to this finding is rejected.

Separate and Unequal

We conclude that in the field of public education the doctrine of "separate but equal" has no place. Separate educational facilities are inherently unequal. Therefore, we hold that the plaintiffs and others similarly situated for whom the actions have been brought are, by reason of the segregation complained of, deprived of the equal protection of the laws guaranteed by the Fourteenth Amendment. This disposition makes unnecessary any discussion whether such segregation also violates the Due Process Clause of the Fourteenth Amendment.

Because these are class actions, because of the wide applicability of this decision, and because of the great variety of local conditions, the formulation of decrees in these cases presents problems of considerable complexity. On reargument, the consideration of appropriate relief was necessarily subordinated to the primary question—the constitutionality of segregation on public education. We have now announced that such segregation is a denial of the equal protection of the laws. In order that we may have the full assistance of the parties in formulating decrees, the cases will be restored to the docket, and the parties are requested to present further argument on Questions 4 and 5 previously propounded by the Court for the reargument this Term. The Attorney General of the United States is again invited to participate. The Attorneys General of the states requiring or permitting segregation in public education will also be permitted to appear as *Amici Curiae* upon request, to do so by September 15, 1954, and submission of briefs by October 1, 1954.

Viewpoint 4

"This unwarranted exercise of power by the Court, contrary to the Constitution, is creating chaos and confusion in the States principally affected."

The Government Should Not Interfere in School Segregation

Southern Manifesto

In 1954 the Supreme Court declared in *Brown v. Board of Education* that the segregation of public schools is unconstitutional. At the same time that the landmark ruling buoyed the hopes of those within the civil rights movement, however, it compelled the more ardent segregationists to launch an offensive. To maintain the Jim Crow status quo, for example, many southern whites employed a variety of legal and political tactics to undermine and circumvent desegregation. One of the most flagrant statements against integration is the rebuttal by southern leaders to the Supreme Court's decision in *Brown.* The Southern Manifesto, reprinted here, states that the Supreme Court has no right to override the authority of the states, or "substitute naked power for established law." In 1956 over one hundred southern senators and representatives signed the Southern Manifesto, promising to resist federal efforts to desegregate the schools.

Southern Manifesto, "Southern Manifesto: Declaration of Constitutional Principles," *Congressional Record*, 84th congress, 2nd session, March 12, 1956.

The unwarranted decision of the Supreme Court in the public school cases is now bearing the fruit always produced when men substitute naked power for established law.

The Founding Fathers gave us a Constitution of checks and balances because they realized the inescapable lesson of history that no man or group of men can be safely entrusted with unlimited power. They framed this Constitution with its provisions for change by amendment in order to secure the fundamentals of government against the dangers of temporary popular passion or the personal predilections of public office-holders.

An Abuse of Power

We regard the decision of the Supreme Court in the school cases as a clear abuse of judicial power. It climaxes a trend in the Federal Judiciary undertaking to legislate, in derogation of the authority of Congress, and to encroach upon the reserved rights of the States and the people.

The original Constitution does not mention education. Neither does the 14th amendment nor any other amendment. The debates preceding the submission of the 14th amendment clearly show that there was no intent that it should affect the system of education maintained by the States.

The very Congress which proposed the amendment subsequently provided for segregated schools in the District of Columbia.

When the amendment was adopted in 1868, there were 37 States of the Union. Every one of the 26 States that had any substantial racial differences among its people, either approved the operation of segregated schools already in existence or subsequently established such schools by action of the same lawmaking body which considered the 14th amendment.

As admitted by the Supreme Court in the public school case (*Brown v. Board of Education*), the doctrine of separate but equal schools "apparently originated in *Roberts v. City of Boston* (1849), upholding school segregation against attack as being violative of a State constitutional guarantee of equality." This constitutional doctrine began in the North, not in the South, and it was followed not only in Massachusetts, but in Connecticut, New York, Illinois, Indiana, Michigan, Minnesota, New Jersey, Ohio, Pennsylvania and other northern States until they, exercising their rights as States through the constitutional processes of local self-government, changed their school systems.

In the case of *Plessy v. Ferguson* in 1896 the Supreme Court expressly declared that under the 14th amendment no person was denied any of his rights if the States provided separate but equal public facilities. This decision has been followed in many other cases. It is notable that the Supreme Court, speaking through Chief Justice [William H.] Taft, a former President of the United States, unanimously declared in 1927 in *Lum v. Rice* that the "separate but equal" principle is "within the discretion of the State in regulating its public schools and does not conflict with the 14th amendment."

This interpretation, restated time and again, became a part of the life of the people of many of the States and confirmed their habits, customs, traditions, and way of life. It is founded on elemental humanity and commonsense, for parents should not be deprived by Government of the right to direct the lives and education of their own children.

Though there has been no constitutional amendment or act of Congress changing this established legal principle almost a century old, the Supreme Court of the United States, with no legal basis for such action, undertook to exercise their naked judicial power and substituted their personal political and social ideas for the established law of the land.

This unwarranted exercise of power by the Court, contrary to the Constitution, is creating chaos and confusion in the States principally affected. It is destroying the amicable relations between the white and Negro races that have been created through 90 years of patient effort by the good people of both races. It has planted hatred and suspicion where there has been heretofore friendship and understanding.

Without regard to the consent of the governed, outside agitators are threatening immediate and revolutionary changes in our public-school systems. If done, this is certain to destroy the system of public education in some of the States.

With the gravest concern for the explosive and dangerous condition created by this decision and inflamed by outside meddlers:

We reaffirm our reliance on the Constitution as the fundamental law of the land.

We decry the Supreme Court's encroachments on rights re-

Statement and Proclamation of Governor George C. Wallace

Among those who gained notoriety for their white supremacist views was Alabama governor George C. Wallace, who won his 1962 gubernatorial campaign with promises to defend the state's right to maintain segregation in its schools. Months after his inauguration, Wallace had a chance to fulfill his pledge. On June 11, 1963, Wallace read his proclamation, excerpted here, as he attempted to block two black students from entering the University of Alabama. The governor stepped aside only when the federalized Alabama National Guard arrived.

The unwelcomed, unwanted, unwarranted and force-induced intrusion upon the campus of the University of Alabama today of the might of the Central Government offers frightful example of the oppression of the rights, privileges and sovereignty of this State by officers of the Federal Government. This intrusion results solely from force, or threat of force, undignified by any reasonable application of the principle of law, reason and justice. It is important that the people of this State and nation understand that this action is in violation of rights reserved to the State by the Constitution of the United States and the Constitution of the State of Alabama. While some few may applaud these acts, millions of Americans will gaze in sorrow upon the situation existing at this great institution of learning.

Only the Congress makes the law of the United States. To this date no statutory authority can be cited to the people of this Country which authorizes the Central Government to ignore the sovereignty of this State in an attempt to subordinate the rights of Alabama amid millions of Americans. There has been no legislative action by Congress justifying this intrusion.

served to the States and to the people, contrary to established law, and to the Constitution.

We commend the motives of those States which have declared

When the Constitution of the United States was enacted, a government was formed upon the premise that people, as individuals are endowed with the rights of life, liberty, and property, and with the right of self-government. The people and their local self-governments formed a Central Government and conferred upon it certain stated and limited powers. All other powers were reserved to the states and to the people.

Strong local government is the foundation of our system and must be continually guarded and maintained. The Tenth Amendment to the Constitution of the United States reads as follows:

> "The powers not delegated to the United States by the Constitution, nor prohibited by it to the States, are reserved to the states respectively, or to the people."

This amendment sustains the right of self-government and grants the State of Alabama the right to enforce its laws and regulate its internal affairs.

This nation was never meant to be a unit of one . . . but a united [sic] of the many . . . this is the exact reason our freedom loving forefathers established the states, so as to divide the rights and powers among the states, insuring that no central power could gain master government control.

There can be no submission to the theory that the Central Government is anything but a servant of the people. We are a God-fearing people—not government-fearing people. We practice today the free heritage bequeathed to us by the Founding Fathers.

"Statement and Proclamation of George C. Wallace," University of Alabama, June 11, 1963.

the intention to resist forced integration by any lawful means.

We appeal to the States and people who are not directly affected by these decisions to consider the constitutional principles involved against the time when they too, on issues vital to them, may be the victims of judicial encroachment.

Even though we constitute a minority in the present Congress, we have full faith that a majority of the American people believe in the dual system of government which has enabled us to achieve our greatness and will in time demand that the reserved rights of the States and of the people be made secure against judicial usurpation.

We pledge ourselves to use all lawful means to bring about a reversal of this decision which is contrary to the Constitution and to prevent the use of force in its implementation.

In this trying period, as we all seek to right this wrong, we appeal to our people not to be provoked by the agitators and trouble-makers invading our States and to scrupulously refrain from disorder and lawless acts.

"Brown set the modern stage for us to begin building an America which fulfills its promise of equality and justice for blacks and other minorities."

Brown v. Board of Education Boosted Civil Rights

Julius L. Chambers

The Supreme Court's landmark decision in *Brown v. Board of Education* has been hailed by many as the most important ruling of the twentieth century. Attorney Julius L. Chambers is among those who finds *Brown* "one of this civilization's proudest achievements." In the short term, the *Brown* ruling boosted black educational opportunities by eradicating segregation in the classroom. On a larger scale, and perhaps more importantly, the legal precedents set forth in *Brown* shaped the civil rights movement for decades to come.

At the same time, *Brown* has weathered much criticism—most notably from opponents who view the decision as an ineffectual vehicle for the promotion of racial justice. Chambers warns against this tendency to denigrate *Brown* against a "thicket of revisionist historical arguments." According to Chambers, *Brown*,

Julius L. Chambers, "*Brown v. Board of Education*," *Race in America: The Struggle for Equality*, edited by Herbert Hill and James E. Jones. Madison: University of Wisconsin Press, 1993. Copyright © 1993 by The Board of Regents of the University of Wisconsin System. All rights reserved. Reproduced by permission.

whatever its limitations, cannot be held responsible for all the impediments—which have been fueled by three centuries of racial oppression—that continue to affect black and other minority schoolchildren. Chambers is a civil rights attorney, activist, and educator. He lectures at many law schools and has written numerous articles and books on civil rights.

The quality and moral worth of any civilization should be measured by the ability of all of its citizens to fulfill their potential, to be the best that they can be. And given that definition, when we consider the vast numbers of minority children who lack even the hope of gaining the basic tools needed to be productive and fulfilled citizens, it is easy to feel that this "American civilization" is a contradiction in terms.

But many of us do not believe that. Many of us have not given up the dream of equal opportunity and equal rights for all citizens. For us, one of this civilization's proudest achievements is the *Brown v. Board of Education* decision. I believe that, for all of its flaws, for all that it did not accomplish, *Brown* set the modern stage for us to begin building an America which fulfills its promise of equality and justice for blacks and other minorities. If we spend a moment reflecting on what we *thought* Brown had achieved in those heady days in the mid-fifties and then look at what we have *actually* achieved, it will help us define the work that remains to be done, as we try to shape an American civilization we would like our children and grandchildren to be part of.

When *Brown* was decided, I was a young teenager in a small, segregated high school in rural North Carolina. I remember gathering with my schoolmates and teachers after class and celebrating. As lay people, we sincerely believed that *Brown* marked the end of the unequal, inadequate education provided to blacks throughout the South. We honestly thought that blacks would suddenly be able to attend the schools of their choice, the "good" white schools, or previously black schools that would be improved. We thought that we would get access to better facilities, and have a much better chance to make something of ourselves. If we thought about the nature of law at all, we assumed that

Brown was self-executing. The law had been announced, and now people would have to obey it. Wasn't that how things worked in America, even in white America?

Brown's Limitations

That kind of naivete was not limited to the children and adults of Montgomery County, North Carolina. It also extended to many of the civil rights lawyers who fought to make *Brown* possible. They believed, correctly, I think, that segregated education was the weak link in the chain of laws that maintained all separate facilities for southern blacks. Once that link was broken, they assumed, the entire chain would collapse. But many of them took their exultation one step further: they also believed that racism itself would vanish. Once "separate but equal" was no longer the law of the land, separate and unequal would stop being a fact of everyday life. Once blacks and whites started learning together, they would start living together, working together, building a society where race did not limit destiny.

At the time, only a few isolated voices in the black community called attention to *Brown*'s serious limitations. W.E.B. Du Bois understood that integration alone could not be equated with quality education. He knew that integration alone could not solve the persistent, daunting educational and emotional problems of many urban and rural black students, problems that were the direct result of poverty and continuing racism. A few others pointed out what eventually became abundantly clear: even if the often passionate and violent resistance to southern school desegregation could be overcome, even if the Little Rocks and the Birminghams could be integrated, it would not necessarily change increasingly segregated housing patterns in the rest of the country. And those segregated housing patterns—with largely minority central cities and largely white suburbs—would perpetuate unequal education. Nor would school integration alone necessarily change persistent racism.

Nevertheless, those voices were few and far between at the time. And today, hindsight being 20/20, one doesn't have to be an educational expert to see that much of what Du Bois said was true, and that the dreams and expectations of so many of us after *Brown* have been confounded. My friend Derrick Bell and others have argued, quite persuasively, that *Brown* and related Court decisions have only served the interests of the white majority. Since the decision did not really address Du Bois' concern, did not focus on the complex set of barriers that black students must overcome to have productive futures, it only served to siphon off conveniently and painlessly the discontent of minorities. *Brown*, the argument goes, gave blacks enough legal crumbs to satisfy them for a time, while the rest of America continued its feast.

But I believe that this argument is faulty when it implies that the Court in *Brown should* have addressed all the barriers and problems that it did not address. The Court was hewing to its traditional role of making decisions on the basis of the facts and circumstances of the case before it. In that case, the conclusion it reached was patently obvious and remains true today: segregated schooling is inherently unequal, because it inevitably results in the unequal distribution of educational resources. In taking steps to end that segregation, the Court could not possibly have addressed *all* the impediments that have prevented millions of minority youngsters from getting an adequate education. Only a visionary like Du Bois was able to see those impediments clearly, and unfortunately visionaries are often taken seriously only after they have left us.

Yet as much as we should respect Du Bois for his contributions to this ongoing argument, I believe his ultimate conclusion—putting most of our priorities on improving black institutions, at the expense of integration—was wrong. [There are] barriers we must still overcome in order to fulfill the dreams and expectations that *Brown* created. But first, it is important to assert that the failure to meet those expectations should not lead us to conclude that the goals enunciated in *Brown* were misguided, or even based on false hopes. It is important that we do not lose sight of one principle amidst the thicket of revisionist historical arguments about *Brown:* integrated schools *do* improve the educational opportunities available to black students. And in doing so, integrated schools contribute a great deal to the social and economic progress that should be the goal of all races.

We must not overlook the studies by Professor Robert L. Crain at Columbia University and others which show that the earlier black students are exposed to integrated educational settings, the more impressive their gains in raising scholastic achievements. Crain has shown that one-fifth of the achievement gap between black and white students disappears within the first two years of school integration. Other studies, cited in the National Research Council's *A Common Destiny*, show that blacks attending desegregated schools are more likely to attend desegregated institutions of higher learning. And they are more likely than blacks from majority-black schools to major in scientific and technical fields. Without simplifying or glossing over the problems that confront us, it is vital for us not to lose sight of the fact that school integration has many, varied, and positive outcomes for minority students.

But the benefits of integration are not limited to minorities. They also extend to that white power structure with which Derrick Bell is so concerned. Many of the corporate leaders with whom I come in contact understand that blacks and other minorities will constitute 40 percent of our workforce by the year 2000. And they know that it is in their interest to make sure that our children are adequately trained, if only to keep the engines of capitalism running. Since the data show that integrated education is one key to quality education—though certainly not the only key—corporate America is just beginning to understand its value.

And finally, integrated education remains the best way to prepare all students—both black and white—for the complex, multicultural, multiracial society which they'll soon be joining. Studies show that students in desegregated schools are more likely to live, work, and develop friendships with people of different races.

That is why continuing to walk on the path of integration that started with *Brown* is crucial not only to blacks, but to all Americans. Again, the solution offered by *Brown* is certainly no panacea. . . . But it is important to note that, right now, one of the principal threats to quality education for all is the growing resegregation of America's public schools.

Resegregation

More children attend racially isolated schools today than in the early seventies. Almost two-thirds of minority elementary and secondary students attend schools in which minorities make up more than half the student body. Nearly one-fifth attend schools in which 99 to 100 percent of the students are minorities.

I'm sure I don't need to dwell on the obvious: this educational segregation is generally a direct result of economics and of housing segregation, problems *Brown* did not address. It is not uncommon for a single metropolitan area to have 40 or more school districts, with a vastly disproportionate concentration of blacks—many of whom are poor—in the central city, and a disproportionate concentration of whites in the suburbs.

Now, you'd think that a government trying to build the kind of civilization in which we want to live would make efforts both to integrate schools effectively and to help minorities and the poor escape from the substandard, segregated inner-city housing that is a major factor in school segregation today. Yet our federal and local governments have used housing patterns and poverty as excuses for inaction when it comes to school integration. There has been essentially no progress in urban-suburban school desegregation on the national level since the *Milliken v. Bradley* decision in 1974. In that ruling, the Supreme Court struck down a lower court decision ordering the busing of children across district lines as the only practicable way to achieve meaningful integration in the Detroit metropolitan area.

Additionally, in recent years, the Justice Department and many lower courts have quite openly tried to undermine many successful desegregation plans, especially in the South. Increasingly, courts are ruling that racial imbalances in the schools are the result of segregated housing or demographic trends, not the vestiges of past discrimination. With the support of the Justice Department, more and more school districts are trying to take advantage of these rulings and are asking the courts to declare that they have achieved unitary status—which means that courts consider that the districts have already eliminated past discrimination and are operating desegregated schools. Once school districts achieve this so-called unitary status, they no longer have the legal duty to eliminate the continuing vestiges of their racially dual school systems, and black plaintiffs have to prove "intentional discrimination" to obtain relief. Thus, with a unitary-status declaration, school systems can literally ignore the problems that disproportionately affect black and poor children and can easily return to the segregated patterns of the past.

In early 1988, the Justice Department announced that it would seek to dismiss nearly 300 school desegregation suits and dissolve injunctions requiring school districts to maintain desegregation. The pretext for the federal action was that these districts were unitary.

Fortunately, thanks to a great many dedicated civil rights attorneys, the Justice Department has had only limited success thus far. But the department under the [George H.W.] Bush administration has not stopped this assault on integrated education.

In the face of these trends, a major part of our efforts must be directed toward preserving past gains and to continuing litigation that will effectively integrate all schools—urban, suburban and rural. Although I have noted that there has been no major nationwide progress in this area, the NAACP Legal Defense Fund has won several important desegregation suits. In Natchez, Mississippi, for example, formerly all-black and predominately white schools were consolidated in 1989. And the school district there was integrated after the local school board had fought against desegregation for two decades.

But obviously, preserving and increasing integration is only one part of the job. To fulfill the dreams and expectations we had after *Brown*, we must move beyond *Brown*. That means rectifying the complex set of problems created by three centuries of racial oppression, and the remaining vestiges of a system which at one time legally denied most blacks the right to *any* education. That means overcoming the diverse barriers to equal educational opportunities that perhaps were not wholly understood in 1954. . . .

Thirty-five years after *Brown*, I am not content with simply criticizing *Brown*'s failures or its incomplete implementation. I see too many black and poor children crying every day for an opportunity to learn and to succeed. I also see a country on the brink of more racial and economic strife, with both federal and state governmental entities neglecting their duties and responsibilities under the Constitution. It is incumbent on all of us to play whatever role we can, in whatever forum, to fulfill the dream of *Brown* and the Constitution. For me, that means the continued pursuit of efforts to enforce *Brown*. To others, it may mean using other forums. Whatever approach we choose, I remain optimistic that the dreams we once had in that little classroom in North Carolina eventually will become a reality. And that all of us, in the words of Justice Marshall, will witness an American society where the poor black kid in Mississippi or Harlem or Watts will have the same educational opportunity as the rich white kid of Stamford, Connecticut.

Viewpoint 6

"Brown represents a failed decision in the long term because it helped shape certain ideas about racial identity that proved to be ultimately self-defeating."

Brown v. Board of Education Failed to Promote Civil Rights

Louis Anthes

It is commonly believed that the Supreme Court's 1954 decision in *Brown v. Board of Education*, which declared segregated schools unconstitutional, was a landmark event in the struggle to integrate blacks into the American mainstream. In the following viewpoint, Louis Anthes rejects this assessment. Instead, he argues that the *Brown* decision was ineffective in the short term and counterproductive in the long term. Despite the decision, Anthes points out, the schools remained segregated well into the 1960s. When segregation did finally occur, he adds, it was the result not of *Brown* but of the efforts of grassroots activists. In addition, because the ruling characterized blacks as victimized individuals rather than as an oppressed group, it opened the door for critics of affirmative action policies designed to correct systemic discrimination in America. Anthes is

Louis Anthes, "In the Short Term *Brown* Did Not Help African-Americans Achieve True Equality, and in the Long Term It Has Become Implicated in the Reaction Against Affirmative Action," *History in Dispute, Vol. 2: American Social and Political Movements, 1945–2000: Pursuit of Liberty,* edited by Robert J. Allen. Detroit: St. James Press, 2000. Copyright © 2000 by The Gale Group, Inc. Reproduced by permission.

a scholar of U.S. legal history and the author of *Lawyers and Immigrants, 1870–1940: A Cultural History.*

*B*rown v. *Board of Education of Topeka, Kansas* (1954) was the result of a long-standing legal campaign waged by the National Association for the Advancement of Colored People (NAACP), and its legal arm, the Legal Defense Fund (LDF), to remedy the effects of Jim Crow laws, which segregated public facilities along racial lines throughout many southern states. Starting in the 1930s, the NAACP, led by Thurgood Marshall and Charles Hamilton Houston, sued state and local governments using the Supreme Court's decision in *Plessy* v. *Ferguson* (1896), which had held that Jim Crow laws did not inherently violate the Equal Protection Clause of the Fourteenth Amendment. *Plessy*'s doctrine—known as "separate but equal"—helped to legitimate poor physical maintenance of black public institutions, low pay for black public workers, and dismal employment prospects for blacks. At first Marshall and the NAACP tried to enforce the "separate but equal" doctrine by bringing suits against governments to make them equally support segregated public facilities. This strategy of enforcing *Plessy*, however, increasingly seemed impractical. Therefore, NAACP lawyers began focusing on overturning *Plessy* itself.

By the late 1940s, following a series of legal victories for the NAACP in which the Supreme Court ruled that racial segregation related to election primaries (*Smith* v. *Allwright* in 1944), housing (*Shelley* v. *Kraemer* in 1948), and law school admissions (*Sweatt* v. *Painter* in 1950) was unconstitutional, Marshall turned his attention to public schools. At the time few public schools were integrated in many of the districts straddling the Ohio River and Mason-Dixon Line. In states further south, almost all public schools were racially segregated by law. By taking *Brown* to the Supreme Court, Marshall presented to the justices the heroic opportunity to overrule *Plessy* and steer the country on a course toward racial equality under the law. In 1954 the Court embraced the opportunity and made an attempt at ending segregation. Despite good intentions, *Brown* did not meet its authors' expectations.

Short-Term Failure

First, it failed in the short term, because for ten years most public schools in the South remained radically segregated. In North Carolina and Virginia, for instance, less than one-tenth of 1 percent of black children attended desegregated schools seven years after *Brown*. In South Carolina, Alabama, and Mississippi not one black child attended an integrated public grade school in the 1962–1963 school year. One historian, Michael Klarman, characterized the results of *Brown*: "For ten years, 1954–1964, virtually nothing happened."

Part of the reason for *Brown*'s ineffectiveness was that it failed to offer lower courts bold legal remedies to achieve its objectives. *Brown*, in fact, consisted of two separate opinions, referred to as "*Brown I*" and "*Brown II.*" *Brown I* provided the legal, moral, and social-scientific justifications for racial integration of public schools, and, in a much criticized ruling, *Brown II* set forth vague remedies to achieve *Brown I* by declaring that desegregation be pursued "with all deliberate speed." This rhetoric signaled the justice's hope that school districts would develop their own timetables for desegregation that would be consistent with *Brown*. Instead, most school districts did nothing, and in some cases local politicians, most infamously Governor Orval Faubus, cynically stymied the integration of public schools by blaming the Supreme Court for illegitimately interfering in southern institutions. Thus, rather than supplementing the high-minded principles of *Brown I* with detailed legal rules, *Brown II* failed to give lawyers and judges any legal weapons to wield in concrete cases as local school boards and politicans flouted constitutional laws.

Unintended Consequences

Though it may be accurate to say that *Brown* eventually contributed to desegregation of public schools by the late 1960s and early 1970s, it is also true that such change was not directly the result of the action of the Court, and, in fact, largely resulted from grassroots efforts. In particular, the Civil Rights movement fostered dozens of confrontations involving students, demonstrators, troublemakers, police, lawyers, and federal troops. Rather than *Brown*, it was these confrontations that drew the attention of television cameras, thereby shocking moderate white voters, most of whom were otherwise deeply indifferent to issues concerning racial justice. Only after President Lyndon B. Johnson signed the 1964 Civil Rights Act, in response to the organized pressure of the leaders of the Civil Rights movement, most prominently Martin Luther King Jr., can one observe a clear change in the reporting of the racial make-up of formerly segregated schools. In this light, *Brown*'s beneficial consequences appear unintended, as the decision helped to foster the dramatic, and often brutal, conflicts from which eventually emerged political support for the desegregation of public schools.

Second, *Brown* failed because it helped focus Northern attention away from itself and toward the South, thereby obscuring how suburban development in the North fostered its own patterns of racial segregation. By changing property, zoning, and tax laws, northern voters intensified school segregation in the late 1960s through the 1970s and 1980s—at the same time politicians devised a vocabulary to name urban spaces inhabited by African Americans as the "inner city." Though achieved without Jim Crow laws, Northern segregation was indistinguishable from its southern counterpart, except that *Brown*, by itself, provided little equipment to name it as such.

Long-Term Harm

Finally, *Brown* represents a failed decision in the long term because it helped shape certain ideas about racial identity that proved to be ultimately self-defeating. Though intended to accomplish many things, the decision helped portray blacks as powerless and victimized. As argued by historian Daryl Michael Scott, in *Contempt and Pity: Social Policy and the Image of the Damaged Black Psyche, 1880–1996* (1997), *Brown* represented the black mind as "damaged" by racism and racial segregation. Indeed, among Chief Justice Warren's stated reasons for ending segregation was his view that public education helped a child "to adjust normally to his environment." According to Warren, since black schools were legally segregated, and thereby rendered inferior, the law failed to mainstream and normalize black children to American society. According to Scott, "Warren had crafted a psychiatric appeal that subtly but effectively conveyed the plight of the victim without censuring the guilty."

Warren's nod to psychology in his opinion was related to the Supreme Court's intellectual commitment to individualism in the 1950s and 1960s. By talking about racial justice in psychological terms, the Court made it appear that racism mainly resulted in individual pain and suffering rather than collective struggle. Failing to call attention to the shared history of African-Americans resisting slavery and struggling both within and against segregation, Warren caricatured African-Americans as individuals victimized by law. Thus, their difference from whites was judicially rendered as a simple legal difference, the erasure of which promised to effect a liberation of all individual Americans.

By eliding the history of black public institutions and achievements of African-Americans in the name of normalizing individuals through constitutional law, the Supreme Court helped reinforce a broader consensus about individual happiness then dominating postwar American culture. An important and overlooked consequence of this post-*Brown* valorization of the normal and happy individual has been an inability for judges in the last two decades to provide an intellectual bulwark supporting affirmative action against its critics.

Affirmative action represents a conscious attempt to consider race in the redistribution of public resources, but, as its critics readily complain, race-conscious remedies often perpetuate collective racial identities that appear to contradict the goal of rewarding and promoting individual talent. At their worst, critics of affirmative action argue, with *Brown* in mind, that the law should neither discriminate according to race nor acknowledge its political relevance at all. Often they uphold the vision of a "color-blind" Constitution, as Harlan expressed in *Plessy*. They also argue that race hardly matters any longer, or they argue that it has been transformed into something of a collective national identity, which all Americans supposedly share. Supreme Court Justice Antonin Scalia has written in a recent Supreme Court opinion that limited affirmative action: "In the eyes of the government, we are just one race here. It is American." By celebrating American identity in racially explicit terms, critics of affirmative action such as Scalia cynically appropriate *Brown*'s vision of an integrated society. At the same time, however, Scalia's reading of *Brown* is not tortured. His bad-faith appropriations can be read as ironically consistent with *Brown*'s promotion of equality under the Constitution, since the decision elevates as one of its goals the education of normal, individual Americans enjoying the fruits of affluence.

Brown is viewed today as a fixed star in the constellation of American rights. If viewed from another perspective, the most important Supreme Court decision of the twentieth century appears to have had little social effect as intended. It also appears to have disserved African-Americans by hampering the struggle against ways of thinking in racist terms. Therefore, the promotion of racial justice may require going back to *Brown*, reconsidering first principles, and reaching for something deeper than normalizing people into the affluence of an imagined American race.

CHAPTER 3

What Were the Strategies of the Civil Rights Movement?

✹ Chapter Preface

Following the emancipation of the slaves, a variety of individuals and organizations rose to the political fore to advance racial justice and equality. Despite a few significant gains that forced a modicum of change—the creation of constitutional amendments that established citizenship rights and guaranteed voting rights and equal protection of the law, for example—progress in the civil rights arena was slow, if not nonexistent at times. Not until the 1950s, after almost a century of efforts on the part of blacks, would the issue of civil rights become a nationally celebrated cause.

The civil rights movement that blossomed in full force between 1954 and 1965 produced a number of remarkable leaders and organizations committed to the cause of racial justice. During this time of profound upheaval, there was little consensus on how to best secure the rights that had long been denied to black Americans. Some, most notably Thurgood Marshall and the National Association for the Advancement of Colored People, thought that change could be effected only through legal means. Martin Luther King Jr. and the Southern Christian Leadership Conference endorsed nonviolent direct-action campaigns—marches, strikes, and rallies—to draw attention to their cause. At the same time, Malcolm X, Stokely Carmichael, and others came to believe that these strategies were overly cautious and instead advocated more retaliatory and confrontational measures. While some denounced these more militant tactics on the grounds that they would impede the process of integration, others did not want to assimilate into white society at all. Many, indeed, believed that their only chance for enhanced rights lay in the establishment of an African homeland. Still others debated the role of whites in the freedom struggle, the impact of federal legislation, and even the relationship between civil rights and the women's movement. The following chapter represents a small sampling of the wide array of views and opinions that informed and shaped the struggle for civil rights.

Viewpoint 1

"We have a right to expect that the Negro community will be responsible, will uphold the law, but they have a right to expect the law will be fair."

Federal Legislation Will Strengthen Civil Rights

John F. Kennedy

John F. Kennedy's ascendancy to the White House in 1960 generated hope among blacks that the federal government would lend support to the burgeoning civil rights movement. Kennedy, though, took a somewhat moderate stance on racial issues during the first part of his presidency. By 1963, however, pressure for racial equality was mounting, particularly in Alabama, where violent confrontations between demonstrators and police in Birmingham were gaining national attention. At the same time, the state's governor, George Wallace, was making headlines as he attempted to defy the court-ordered integration of the University of Alabama by personally blocking the entrance of two black students.

In response to these highly publicized events, Kennedy took action: On June 11, 1963, the president addressed the issue of civil rights—and rising racial violence—before the American

John F. Kennedy, radio and television address to the American people, June 11, 1963.

public. In his televised speech, excerpted here, Kennedy both endorses the goals of the civil rights movement and proposes federal legislation as a means to racial equality.

G ood evening, my fellow citizens. This afternoon, following a series of threats and defiant statements, the presence of Alabama National Guardsmen was required on the University of Alabama to carry out the final and unequivocal order of the United States District Court of the Northern District of Alabama. That order called for the admission of two clearly qualified young Alabama residents who happened to have been born Negro.

That they were admitted peacefully on the campus is due in good measure to the conduct of the students of the University of Alabama, who met their responsibilities in a constructive way.

I hope that every American, regardless of where he lives, will stop and examine his conscience about this and other related incidents. This Nation was founded by men of many nations and backgrounds. It was founded on the principle that all men are created equal, and that the rights of every man are diminished when the rights of one man are threatened.

Today we are committed to a worldwide struggle to promote and protect the rights of all who wish to be free. And when Americans are sent to Viet-Nam or West Berlin, we do not ask for whites only. It ought to be possible, therefore, for American students of any color to attend any public institution they select without having to be backed up by troops.

It ought to be possible for American consumers of any color to receive equal service in places of public accommodation, such as hotels and restaurants and theaters and retail stores, without being forced to resort to demonstrations in the street, and it ought to be possible for American citizens of any color to register and to vote in a free election without interference or fear of reprisal.

It ought to be possible, in short, for every American to enjoy the privileges of being American without regard to his race or his color. In short, every American ought to have the right to be treated as he would wish to be treated, as one would wish his children to be treated. But this is not the case.

The Negro baby born in America today, regardless of the section of the Nation in which he is born, has about one-half as much chance of completing a high school as a white baby born in the same place on the same day, one-third as much chance of completing college, one-third as much chance of becoming a professional man, twice as much chance of becoming unemployed, about one-seventh as much chance of earning $10,000 a year, a life expectancy which is 7 years shorter, and the prospects of earning only half as much.

This is not a sectional issue. Difficulties over segregation and discrimination exist in every city, in every State of the Union, producing in many cities a rising tide of discontent that threatens the public safety. Nor is this a partisan issue. In a time of domestic crisis men of good will and generosity should be able to unite regardless of party or politics. This is not even a legal or legislative issue alone. It is better to settle these matters in the courts than on the streets, and new laws are needed at every level, but law alone cannot make men see right.

We are confronted primarily with a moral issue. It is as old as the scriptures and is as clear as the American Constitution.

The heart of the question is whether all Americans are to be afforded equal rights and equal opportunities, whether we are going to treat our fellow Americans as we want to be treated. If an American, because his skin is dark, cannot eat lunch in a restaurant open to the public, if he cannot send his children to the best public school available, if he cannot vote for the public officials who represent him, if, in short, he cannot enjoy the full and free life which all of us want, then who among us would be content to have the color of his skin changed and stand in his place? Who among us would then be content with the counsels of patience and delay?

One hundred years of delay have passed since President Lincoln freed the slaves, yet their heirs, their grandsons, are not fully free. They are not yet freed from the bonds of injustice. They are not yet freed from social and economic oppression. And this Nation, for all its hopes and all its boasts, will not be fully free until all its citizens are free.

We preach freedom around the world, and we mean it, and we cherish our freedom here at home, but are we to say to the world, and much more importantly, to each other that this is a land of the free except for the Negroes; that we have no second-class citizens except Negroes; that we have no class or caste system, no ghettoes, no master race except with respect to Negroes?

The Nation's Promise

Now the time has come for this Nation to fulfill its promise. The events in Birmingham and elsewhere have so increased the cries for equality that no city or State or legislative body can prudently choose to ignore them.

The fires of frustration and discord are burning in every city, North and South, where legal remedies are not at hand. Redress is sought in the streets, in demonstrations, parades, and protests which create tensions and threaten violence and threaten lives.

We face, therefore, a moral crisis as a country and as a people. It cannot be met by repressive police action. It cannot be left to increased demonstrations in the streets. It cannot be quieted by token moves or talk. It is a time to act in the Congress, in your State and local legislative body and, above all, in all of our daily lives.

It is not enough to pin the blame on others, to say this is a problem of one section of the country or another, or deplore the fact that we face. A great change is at hand, and our task, our obligation, is to make that revolution, that change, peaceful and constructive for all.

Those who do nothing are inviting shame as well as violence. Those who act boldly are recognizing right as well as reality.

Next week I shall ask the Congress of the United States to act, to make a commitment it has not fully made in this century to the proposition that race has no place in American life or law. The Federal judiciary has upheld that proposition in a series of forthright cases. The executive branch has adopted that proposition in the conduct of its affairs, including the employment of Federal personnel, the use of Federal facilities, and the sale of federally financed housing.

But there are other necessary measures which only the Congress can provide, and they must be provided at this session. The old code of equity law under which we live commands for every wrong a remedy, but in too many communities, in too many parts of the country, wrongs are inflicted on Negro citizens and there are no remedies at law. Unless the Congress acts, their only remedy is in the street.

A Call for Legislation

I am, therefore, asking the Congress to enact legislation giving all Americans the right to be served in facilities which are open to the public—hotels, restaurants, theaters, retail stores, and similar establishments.

This seems to me to be an elementary right. Its denial is an arbitrary indignity that no American in 1963 should have to endure, but many do.

I have recently met with scores of business leaders urging them to take voluntary action to end this discrimination and I have been encouraged by their response, and in the last two weeks over 75 cities have seen progress made in desegregating these kinds of facilities. But many are unwilling to act alone, and for this reason, nationwide legislation is needed if we are to move this problem from the streets to the courts.

I am also asking Congress to authorize the Federal Government in participate more fully in lawsuits designed to end segregation in public education. We have succeeded in persuading many districts to desegregate voluntarily. Dozens have admitted Negroes without violence. Today a Negro is attending a State-supported institution in every one of our 50 States, but the pace is very slow.

Too many Negro children entering segregated grade schools at the time of the Supreme Court's decision 9 years ago will enter segregated high schools this fall, having suffered a loss which can never be restored. The lack of an adequate education denies the Negro a chance to get a decent job.

The orderly implementation of the Supreme Court decision, therefore, cannot be left solely to those who may not have the economic resources to carry the legal action or who may be subject to harassment.

Other features will be also requested, including greater protection for the right to vote. But legislation, I repeat, cannot solve this problem alone. It must be solved in the homes of every American in every community across our country.

Praising Civil Rights Workers

In this respect, I want to pay tribute to those citizens North and South who have been working in their communities to make life better for all. They are acting not out of a sense of legal duty but out of a sense of human decency.

Like our soldiers and sailors in all parts of the world they are meeting freedom's challenge on the firing line, and I salute them for their honor and their courage.

My fellow Americans, this is a problem which faces us all—in every city of the North as well as the South. Today there are Negroes unemployed, two or three times as many compared to whites, inadequate in education, moving into the large cities, unable to find work, young people particularly out of work without hope, denied equal rights, denied the opportunity to eat at a restaurant or lunch counter or go to a movie theater, denied the right to a decent education, denied almost today the right to attend a State university even though qualified. It seems to me that these are matters which concern us all, not merely Presidents or Congressmen or Governors, but every citizen of the United States.

This is one country. It has become one country because all of us and all the people who came here had an equal chance to develop their talents.

We cannot say to 10 percent of the population that you can't have that right; that your children can't have the chance to develop whatever talents they have; that the only way that they are going to get their rights is to go into the streets and demonstrate. I think we owe them and we owe ourselves a better country than that.

Therefore, I am asking for your help in making it easier for us to move ahead and to provide the kind of equality of treatment which we would want ourselves; to give a chance for every child to be educated to the limit of his talents.

As I have said before, not every child has an equal talent or an equal ability or an equal motivation, but they should have the equal right to develop their talent and their ability and their motivation, to make something of themselves.

We have a right to expect that the Negro community will be responsible, will uphold the law, but they have a right to expect that the law will be fair, that the Constitution will be color blind, as Justice [John] Harlan said at the turn of the century.

This is what we are talking about and this is a matter which concerns this country and what it stands for, and in meeting it I ask the support of all our citizens.

Thank you very much.

Viewpoint 2

"We can rely upon none but ourselves as a catalyst in the development of the potential power of the black community."

Federal Civil Rights Legislation Is Inadequate

James Farmer

The Congress of Racial Equality (CORE) was founded in 1942 to challenge segregation and discrimination through nonviolent resistance at restaurants, waiting rooms, and other public areas. Despite its pacifist origins, however, CORE evolved with the political climate: As the quest for black rights intensified in the sixties, CORE, under the leadership of Executive Director James Farmer, began to abandon its long-held belief in nonviolent protest and promote a more militant, separatist agenda.

The following is excerpted from Farmer's report on civil rights to the 1965 CORE Convention. For Farmer, the key to enhanced civil rights is not federal legislation or governmental programs. Farmer calls the Civil Rights Acts of 1957, 1960, and 1964, for example, only marginally effective as a tool for the acquisition of greater equality—and certainly not a panacea for the racial ills plaguing the country. Rather, Farmer advocates a

James Farmer, annual report to the CORE Convention, July 1, 1965.

strategy whereby blacks harness their group power through independent political action and community organization.

As CORE meets at its 23rd Annual Convention, we have behind us many successes achieved and victories won. But this report will not be a recounting of past successes; to rest on one's laurels is to atrophy and die. Past victories—in public accommodations, in voting rights, in the support of law and public policy—have been in battles preceding the major encounter.

The major war now confronting us is aimed at harnessing the awesome political potential of the black community in order to effect basic social and economic changes for all Americans, to alter meaningfully the lives of the Black Americans (our plight has not been and will not be changed by past victories), and to bring about a real equality of free men.

This job cannot be done for us by the Government. In the first place, the establishments—Federal, State, and Local—have too much built-in resistance to fundamental change. Any establishment by definition seeks its own perpetuation and rejects that which threatens it. For example, politicians take over and seek to make the anti-poverty programs an adjunct of their political aspirations. They attack community action programs of the anti-poverty war as being anti-city hall. School Boards, which have already lost the drop-outs and other under-privileged youth, reach out greedily to control community education programs and see that they do not shake up the school systems. Powerful lobbies, such as the financial and the real estate interests, exert tremendous pressure to see that programs to relieve poverty do not threaten their interests.

Further, it is impossible for the Government to mount a decisive war against poverty and bigotry in the United States while it is pouring billions down the drain in a war against people in Viet Nam. The billion dollars available to fight poverty is puny compared with the need and insignificant compared with the resources expended in wars.

Thus, we must be constructive critics of the anti-poverty program, using its resources for our fight where we can, insisting that local anti-poverty boards be truly representatives of the deprived communities and the minorities which they are supposed to help, and attacking waste and pork-barreling wherever it occurs.

Yet it would be fatal to think that the anti-poverty program alone can make the necessary changes in the social and economic life of Black Americans. It can be no more a solution to our problems than the Civil Rights Acts of 1957, 1960, 1964 were, or the Voter Rights Act of 1965 will be. Like those laws, the anti-poverty program has to be seen as no more than a tool, useful at times but inadequate at best to do the job.

We can rely upon none but ourselves as a catalyst in the development of the potential power of the black community in its own behalf and in behalf of the nation. CORE alone has the nationwide network of militant chapters required, unshackled by compromising entanglements, political commitments and alliances. CORE alone has the flexibility to move in the new directions demanded by this phase of the war, while it fulfills its commitments to the unfinished tasks of the last phase.

In this new phase of our war to change the life of the Negro in a changed America, there are two aspects: Community organization and Political organization. It must be clearly seen that neither aspect is an end in itself. Community organization, including social services, for its own sake is mere social uplift and has no basic importance in changing the life role of the Negro. Political organization for its own sake is sheer opportunism. While both aspects must be undertaken simultaneously, the first, community organization, may be seen as a step to increase the effectiveness of the second, political organization. Or another way of viewing it, is to see community organization as a tool—a tool to build a vehicle. Political organization, then, is the vehicle to take us to the desired objective. That objective is an open society free of race discrimination and forced segregation, shorn of poverty and unemployment, with decent housing and high-quality education for all. The objective, in a word, is a new society, a free and open society.

Community Organizations

The term, community organization, has become almost a cliché. The need now is to put content into that cliché. For two years, community organization has been widely discussed within CORE. For many, the discussion of it has been a substitute for taking concrete steps to achieve it. Many CORE Chapters, however, have moved their offices into the heart of the black ghetto and have made a serious attempt at ghetto involvement and community organization. If we are honest we will admit that most have failed, though a few have had small successes at organizing their community. Thus the impact of some of our chapters has dwindled. So now, here we stand, faltering for a necessary transition. If the need for community organization has been great in the past, it is now, I believe, desperate. It is now or never. CORE's survival as a viable and relevant organization depends upon it. . . .

Before a community can be organized in a way that is meaningful to the community, we must engage in a dialogue with that community. The indigenous people of a community know their hurts, their needs and their problems far better than we. We must encourage the community to speak, for it has much to say. And we must be prepared to listen. Yet we must not be afraid to talk to the community, for we, too, have something of importance to say growing out of our experience in the movement. The decisions, however, must rest with the people of a community or a neighborhood, for it is their lives to be fulfilled, their dreams to be realized. . . .

Political Organization and Action

It is clear that the objectives we seek—in the wiping out of poverty and unemployment, elimination of bad housing, city planning for integration in housing and schools, quality education—are political objectives depending upon responses we can exact from political machinery. We can no longer rely on pressuring and cajoling political units toward desired actions. We must be in a position of power, a position to change those political units when they are not responsive.

The only way to achieve political objectives is through power, political power. Only diminishing returns can be achieved through the pressure of demonstrations not backed up by political muscle.

We have won amazing successes without political muscle. The

New York City CORE chapters came out against [Emile] Wagner [leader of the staunchly segregationist White Citizens' Council in New Orleans] and the National Director backed them up, and we toppled a Police Commissioner and a Mayor. Now, everyone is a candidate for Mayor and bidding for CORE support. This does not indicate strength. It merely shows what CORE can accomplish in spite of weakness, and thus how much more could be done if we had the political power which can derive from community organization and political organization. . . .

As we organize the community through directed centers, so we must seek to organize the community politically—or, more accurately, to *reorganize* it politically. For the bosses and the machines have already organized it after a fashion with their ward heelers and their petty precinct captains. The greatest tragedy of all would be for the existing black vote to remain in, and the new black vote to be dumped into the general political soup now brewed by the machine bosses—black or white.

What is needed, I believe, is independent political action through indigenous political organizations. This is the Freedom Democratic Party in Mississippi and CORE is supporting it fully, including its challenge. After the Summer CORE Project in Louisiana, if activated communities articulate the desire we will help them organize a Louisiana Freedom Democratic Party.

In the North, independent political voices are needed too. When the black ghetto communities with which CORE chapters have dialogued articulate the desire, we must take the lead in helping them develop Freedom Democratic Movements to serve as a political voice for their awakening self-expression.

Only through such independent action can the growing black vote achieve maximum effectiveness in moving toward the goals we seek. Freedom Democratic Movements must not be racist and should not exclude whites. But their base must be in the black ghetto, else they will be merely another exercise in liberal futility!

Viewpoint 3

"Nonviolence became more than a method to which I gave intellectual assent; it became a commitment to a way of life."

Blacks Must Employ Nonviolent Resistance

Martin Luther King Jr.

A young black preacher named Martin Luther King Jr., took center stage in the civil rights movement when he led the movement to desegregate the city buses in Montgomery, Alabama, in 1955. In the wake of the boycott, King helped found the Southern Christian Leadership Conference (SCLC), a pacifist organization through which King mobilized thousands of demonstrators to voice black grievances. His broad appeal to both whites and blacks was based, in part, on his belief that well organized and executed nonviolence could be a potent weapon against racism, and that the racial divide could be breached only through love.

Throughout his years on the civil rights front—as violent confrontations erupted in Selma, Albany, Birmingham, and other hot spots—King's commitment to nonviolence would be

Martin Luther King Jr., *Stride Toward Freedom: The Montgomery Story*. New York: Harper & Brothers, 1958. Copyright © 1963 by Martin Luther King Jr., copyright renewed 1991 by Coretta Scott King. Reproduced by arrangement with the Estate of Martin Luther King Jr., c/o Writers House as agent for the proprietor New York, NY.

seriously tested. Yet King remained a steadfast proponent of passive resistance until his death, by assassination, in 1968. The following is excerpted from *Stride Toward Freedom*, King's account of the Montgomery bus boycott—and the positive role of nonviolence.

When I went to Montgomery as a pastor, I had not the slightest idea that I would later become involved in a crisis in which nonviolent resistance would be applicable. I neither started the protest nor suggested it. I simply responded to the call of the people for a spokesman. When the protest began, my mind, consciously or unconsciously, was driven back to the Sermon on the Mount, with its sublime teachings on love, and the Gandhian method of nonviolent resistance. As the days unfolded, I came to see the power of nonviolence more and more. Living through the actual experience of the protest, nonviolence became more than a method to which I gave intellectual assent; it became a commitment to a way of life. Many of the things that I had not cleared up intellectually concerning nonviolence were now solved in the sphere of practical action.

The Tenets of Nonviolence

Since the philosophy of nonviolence played such a positive role in the Montgomery Movement, it may be wise to turn to a brief discussion of some basic aspects of this philosophy.

First, it must be emphasized that nonviolent resistance is not a method for cowards; it does resist. If one uses this method because he is afraid or merely because he lacks the instruments of violence, he is not truly nonviolent. This is why Gandhi often said that if cowardice is the only alternative to violence, it is better to fight. He made this statement conscious of the fact that there is always another alternative: no individual or group need submit to any wrong, nor need they use violence to right the wrong; there is the way of nonviolence resistance. This is ultimately the way of the strong man. It is not a method of stagnant passivity. The phrase "passive resistance" often gives the false impression that this is a sort of "do-nothing method" in which the resister quietly and passively accepts evil. But nothing is further from the truth. For while the nonviolent resister is passive in the sense that he is not physically aggressive toward his opponent, his mind and emotions are always active, constantly seeking to persuade his opponent that he is wrong. The method is passive physically, but strongly active spiritually. It is not passive nonresistance to evil, it is active nonviolent resistance to evil.

A second basic fact that characterizes nonviolence is that it does not seek to defeat or humiliate the opponent, but to win his friendship and understanding. The nonviolent resister must often express his protest through noncooperation or boycotts, but he realizes that these are not ends themselves; they are merely means to awaken a sense of moral shame in the opponent. The end is redemption and reconciliation. The aftermath of nonviolence is the creation of the beloved community, while the aftermath of violence is tragic bitterness.

A third characteristic of this method is that the attack is directed against forces of evil rather than against persons who happen to be doing the evil. It is evil that the nonviolent resister seeks to defeat, not the persons victimized by evil. If he is opposing racial injustice, the nonviolent resister has the vision to see that the basic tension is not between races. As I like to say to the people in Montgomery: "The tension in this city is not between white people and Negro people. The tension is, at bottom, between justice and injustice, between the forces of light and the forces of darkness. And if there is a victory, it will be a victory not merely for fifty thousand Negroes, but a victory for justice and the forces of light. We are out to defeat injustice and not white persons who may be unjust."

A fourth point that characterizes nonviolent resistance is a willingness to accept suffering without retaliation, to accept blows from the opponent without striking back. "Rivers of blood may have to flow before we gain our freedom, but it must be our blood," Gandhi said to his countrymen. The nonviolent resister is willing to accept violence if necessary, but never to inflict it. He does not seek to dodge jail. If going to jail is necessary, he enters it "as a bridegroom enters the bride's chamber."

One may well ask: "What is the nonviolent resister's justifica-

Martin Luther King Jr. addresses a crowd of civil rights demonstrators in 1965.
King encourages his followers to support nonviolent protest.

tion for this ordeal to which he invites men, for this mass political application of the ancient doctrine of turning the other cheek?"
The answer is found in the realization that unearned suffering is
redemptive. Suffering, the nonviolent resister realizes, has tremendous educational and transforming possibilities. "Things of fundamental importance to people are not secured by reason alone,
but have to be purchased with their suffering," said Gandhi. He
continues: "Suffering is infinitely more powerful than the law of
the jungle for converting the opponent and opening his ears
which are otherwise shut to the voice of reason."

A fifth point concerning nonviolent resistance is that it avoids
not only external physical violence but also internal violence of
spirit. The nonviolent resister not only refuses to shoot his opponent but he also refuses to hate him. At the center of nonviolence
stands the principle of love. The nonviolent resister would con-

tend that in the struggle for human dignity, the oppressed people of the world must not succumb to the temptation of becoming bitter or indulging in hate campaigns. To retaliate in kind would do nothing but intensify the existence of hate in the universe. Along the way of life, someone must have sense enough and morality enough to cut off the chain of hate. This can only be done by projecting the ethic of love to the center of our lives.

The Power of Love

In speaking of love at this point, we are not referring to some sentimental or affectionate emotion. It would be nonsense to urge men to love their oppressors in an affectionate sense. Love in this connection means understanding, redemptive good will. Here the Greek language comes to our aid. There are three words for love in the Greek New Testament. First, there is *eros*. In Platonic philosophy *eros* meant the yearning of the soul for the realm of the divine. It has come now to mean a sort of aesthetic or romantic love. Second, there is *philia* which means intimate affection between personal friends. *Philia* denotes a sort of reciprocal love; the person loves because he is loved. When we speak of loving those who oppose us, we refer to neither *eros* nor *philia;* we speak of a love which is expressed in the Greek word *agape. Agape* means understanding, redeeming good will for all men. It is an overflowing love which is purely spontaneous, unmotivated, groundless, and creative. It is not set in motion by any quality or function of its object. It is the love of God operating in the human heart.

Agape is disinterested love. It is a love in which the individual seeks not his own good, but the good of his neighbor (I Cor. 10:24). *Agape* does not begin by discriminating between worthy and unworthy people, or any qualities people possess. It begins by loving others *for their sakes.* It is an entirely "neighbor-regarding concern for others," which discovers the neighbor in every man it meets. Therefore, *agape* makes no distinction between friend and enemy; it is directed toward both. If one loves an individual merely on account of his friendliness, he loves him for the sake of the benefits to be gained from the friendship, rather than for the friend's own sake. Consequently, the best way to assure oneself that Love is disinterested is to have love for the enemy-neighbor from whom you can expect no good in return, but only hostility and persecution. Another basic point about *agape* is that it springs from the *need* of the other person—his need for belonging to the best in the human family. The Samaritan who helped the Jew on the Jericho Road was "good" because he responded to the human need that he was presented with. God's love is eternal and fails not because man needs his love. St. Paul assures us that the loving act of redemption was done "while we were yet sinners"—that is, at the point of our greatest need for love. Since the white man's personality is greatly distorted by segregation, and his soul is greatly scarred, he needs the love of the Negro. The Negro must love the white man, because the white man needs his love to remove his tensions, insecurities, and fears.

Agape is not a weak, passive love. It is love in action. *Agape* is love seeking to preserve and create community. It is insistence on community even when one seeks to break it. *Agape* is a willingness to sacrifice in the interest of mutuality. *Agape* is a willingness to go to any length to restore community. It doesn't stop at the first mile, but it goes the second mile to restore community. It is a willingness to forgive, not seven times, but seventy times seven to restore community. The cross is the eternal expression of the length to which God will go in order to restore broken community. The resurrection is a symbol of God's triumph over all the forces that seek to block community. The Holy Spirit is the continuing community creating reality that moves through history. He who works against community is working against the whole of creation. Therefore, if I respond to hate with a reciprocal hate I do nothing but intensify the cleavage in broken community. I can only close the gap in broken community by meeting hate with love. If I meet hate with hate, I become depersonalized, because creation is so designed that my personality can only be fulfilled in the context of community. Booker T. Washington was right: "Let no man pull you so low as to make you hate him." When he pulls you that low he brings you to the point of working against community; he drags you to the point of defying creation, and thereby becoming depersonalized.

In the final analysis, *agape* means a recognition of the fact that all life is interrelated. All humanity is involved in a single process, and all men are brothers. To the degree that I harm my brother, no matter what he is doing to me, to that extent I am harming myself. For example, white men often refuse federal aid to education in order to avoid giving the Negro his rights; but because all men are brothers they cannot deny Negro children without harming their own. They end, all efforts to the contrary, by hurting themselves. Why is this? Because men are brothers. If you harm me, you harm yourself. Love, *agape*, is the only cement that can hold this broken community together. When I am commanded to love, I am commanded to restore community, to resist injustice, and to meet the needs of my brothers.

Faith in One Future

A sixth basic fact about nonviolent resistance is that it is based on the conviction that the universe is on the side of justice. Consequently, the believer in nonviolence has deep faith in the future. This faith is another reason why the nonviolent resister can accept suffering without retaliation. For he knows that in his struggle for justice he has cosmic companionship. It is true that there are devout believers in nonviolence who find it difficult to believe in a personal God. But even these persons believe in the existence of some creative force that works for universal wholeness. Whether we call it an unconscious process, an impersonal Brahman, or a Personal Being of matchless power and infinite love, there is a creative force in this universe that works to bring the disconnected aspects of reality into a harmonious whole.

Viewpoint 4

"When I say fight for independence right here, I don't mean any non-violent fight, or turn-the-other-cheek fight. Those days are gone."

Nonviolent Resistance Is Not Enough

Malcolm X

Following the initial gains and boundless expectations of the early civil rights years, the mid-sixties gave rise to a growing faction of blacks frustrated with the slow pace of the movement. Moreover, whereas early civil rights struggles targeted southern racial practices, focus soon shifted to northern urban communities, where de facto segregation continued to affect housing, education, and employment opportunities. Police brutality, too, was rampant.

The subsequent debate about solutions to the nation's racial problems brought new leaders to prominence, most notably Malcolm X. A charismatic and provocative speaker, Malcolm X, perhaps more than any other civil rights leader, gave voice to the black nationalist fervor which was emerging in northern communities. In 1964, Malcolm delivered the following speech in which he advocates the use of any means necessary to secure black eco-

Malcolm X, "Address to a Meeting in New York, 1964," *Documentary History of the Modern Civil Rights Movement*, edited by Peter B. Levy. Westport, CT: Greenwood Press, 1992. Copyright © 1992 by Peter B. Levy. All rights reserved. Reproduced by permission of Greenwood Publishing Group, Westport, CT.

nomic and political independence from a crippling white power structure. Malcolm X was assassinated the following year.

F riends and enemies, tonight I hope that we can have a little fireside chat with as few sparks as possible tossed around. Especially because of the very explosive condition that the world is in today. Sometimes, when a person's house is on fire and someone comes in yelling fire, instead of the person who is awakened by the yell being thankful, he makes the mistake of charging the one who awakened him with having set the fire. I hope that this little conversation tonight about the black revolution won't cause many of you to accuse us of igniting it when you find it at your doorstep.

I'm still a Muslim, that is, my religion is still Islam. I still believe that there is no god but Allah and that Mohammed is the apostle of Allah. That just happens to be my personal religion. But in the capacity which I am functioning in today, I have no intention of mixing my religion with the problems of 22,000,000 black people in this country. . . .

Black Nationalism

I'm still a Muslim, but I'm also a nationalist, meaning that my political philosophy is black nationalism, my economic philosophy is black nationalism, my social philosophy is black nationalism. And when I say that this philosophy is black nationalism, to me this means that the political philosophy for black nationalism is that which is designed to encourage our people, the black people, to gain complete control over the politics and the politicians of our own people.

Our economic philosophy is that we should gain economic control over the economy of our own community, the businesses and the other things which create employment so that we can provide jobs for our own people instead of having to picket and boycott and beg someone else for a job.

And, in short, our social philosophy means that we feel that it is time to get together among our own kind and eliminate the evils that are destroying the moral fiber of our society, like drug addiction, drunkenness, adultery that leads to an abundance of bastard children, welfare problems. We believe that we should lift the level or the standard of our own society to a higher level wherein we will be satisfied and then not inclined toward pushing ourselves into other societies where we are not wanted. . . .

Just as we can see that all over the world one of the main problems facing the West is race, likewise here in America today, most of your Negro leaders as well as the whites agree that 1964 itself appears to be one of the most explosive years yet in the history of America on the racial front, on the racial scene. Not only is the

Marcus Garvey and the Universal Negro Improvement Association

Long before leaders like Malcolm X or Stokely Carmichael rose to the political fore, Marcus Garvey, and the Universal Negro Improvement Association that he founded in 1914, exhorted blacks to take pride in their heritage and resist assimilation into mainstream America. Garvey's paramount goal, moreover, was the creation of a separate black nation, an idea that prefigured the black nationalist movement that would come to prominence in the sixties. The following statement by Garvey is excerpted from The Philosophy and Opinions of Marcus Garvey.

Generally the public is kept misinformed of the truth surrounding new movements of reform. Very seldom, if ever, reformers get the truth told about them and their movements. Because of this natural attitude, the Universal Negro Improvement Association has been greatly handicapped in its work, causing thereby one of the most liberal and helpful human movements of the twentieth century to be held up to ridicule by those who take pride in poking fun at anything not already successfully established.

The white man of America has become the natural leader of the world. He, because of his exalted position, is called upon to help in all human efforts. From nations to individuals the racial explosion probably to take place in America, but all of the ingredients for this racial explosion in America to blossom into a world-wide racial explosion present themselves right here in front of us. America's racial powder keg, in short, can actually fuse or ignite a world-wide powder keg.

And whites in this country who are still complacent when they see the possibilities of racial strife getting out of hand and you are complacent simply because you think you outnumber the racial minority in this country, what you have to bear in mind is wherein

---

appeal is made to him for aid in all things affecting humanity, so, naturally, there can be no great mass movement or change without first acquainting the leader on whose sympathy and advice the world moves.

It is because of this, and more so because of a desire to be Christian friends with the white race, why I explain the aims and objects of the Universal Negro Improvement Association.

The Universal Negro Improvement Association was an organization among Negroes that was seeking to improve the condition of the race, with the view of establishing a nation in Africa where Negroes would be given the opportunity to develop by themselves, without creating the hatred and animosity that now exist in countries of the white race through Negroes rivaling them for the highest and best positions in government, politics, society and industry. The organization believes in the rights of all men, yellow, white and black. To us, the white race has a right to the peaceful possession and occupation of countries of its own and in like manner the yellow and black races have their rights. It is only by an honest and liberal consideration of such rights can the world be blessed with the peace that is sought by Christian teachers and leaders.

Marcus Garvey, *The Philosophy and Opinions of Marcus Garvey.* New York: Universal Publishing House, 1923.

you might outnumber us in this country, you don't outnumber us all over the earth.

Any kind of racial explosion that takes place in this country today, in 1964, is not a racial explosion that can be confined to the shores of America. It is a racial explosion that can ignite the racial powder keg that exists all over the planet that we call the earth. Now I think that nobody would disagree that the dark masses of Africa and Asia and Latin America are already seething with bitterness, animosity, hostility, unrest; and impatience with the racial intolerance that they themselves have experienced at the hands of the white West.

Malcolm X

And just as they themselves have the ingredients of hostility toward the West in general, here we also have 22,000,000 African-Americans, black, brown, red, and yellow people in this country who are also seething with bitterness and impatience and hostility and animosity at the racial intolerance not only of the white West but of white America in particular. . . .

1964 will be America's hottest year; her hottest year yet; a year of much racial violence and much racial bloodshed. But it won't be blood that's going to flow only on one side. The new generation of black people that have grown up in this country during recent years are already forming the opinion, and it's just opinion, that if there is to be bleeding, it should be reciprocal—bleeding on both sides. . . .

So today, when the black man starts reaching out for what America says are his rights, the black man feels that he is within his rights—when he becomes the victim of brutality by those who are depriving him of his rights—to do whatever necessary to protect himself. . . .

There are 22,000,000 African-Americans who are ready to fight for independence right here. When I say fight for independence right here, I don't mean any non-violent fight, or turn-the-other-cheek fight. Those days are gone. Those days are over.

The Lessons of History

If George Washington didn't get independence for this country nonviolently, and if Patrick Henry didn't come up with a non-violent statement, and you taught me to look upon them as patriots and heroes, then it's time for you to realize that I have studied your books well. . . .

Every time a black man gets ready to defend himself some Uncle Tom tries to tell us, how can you win? That's Tom talking. Don't listen to him This is the first thing we hear: the odds are against you. You're dealing with black people who don't care anything about odds. . . .

Again I go back to the people who founded and secured the independence of this country from the colonial power of England. . . . They didn't care about the odds. . . .

Our people are becoming more politically mature. . . . The Negro can see that he holds the balance of power in this country politically. It is he who puts in office the one who gets in office. Yet when the Negro helps that person get in office the Negro gets nothing in return. . . .

The present administration, the Democratic administration, has been there for four years. Yet no meaningful legislation has been passed by them that proposes to benefit black people in this country, despite the fact that in the House they have 267 Democrats and only 177 Republicans. . . . In the Senate there are 67 Democrats and only 33 Republicans. The Democrats control two thirds of the government and it is the Negroes who put them in a position to control the government. Yet they give the Negroes nothing in return but a few handouts in the form of appointments that are only used as window-dressing to make it appear that the problem is being solved.

No, something is wrong. And when these black people wake up and find out for real the trickery and the treachery that has been heaped upon us you are going to have revolution. And when I say revolution I don't mean that stuff they were talking about last year about "We Shall Overcome.". . .

And the only way without bloodshed that this [revolution] can be brought about is that the black man has to be given full use of the ballot in every one of the 50 states. But if the black man doesn't get the ballot, then you are going to be faced with another man who forgets the ballot and starts using the bullet. . . .

So you have a people today who not only know what they want, but also know what they are supposed to have. And they themselves are clearing the way for another generation that is coming up that not only will know what it wants and know what it should have, but also will be ready and willing to do whatever is necessary to see what they should have materializes immediately. Thank you.

Viewpoint 5

"Our concern for black power addresses itself directly to . . . the necessity to reclaim our history and our identity."

Blacks Should Strive for Black Power

Stokely Carmichael

The civil rights movement entered a new phase in the later part of the 1960s, when "black power" became the rallying cry of black militant groups across the country. Leading this new movement was Stokely Carmichael, the fiery young leader of the Student Nonviolent Coordinating Committee (SNCC). Carmichael first popularized black power—and ignited great controversy—when he used the term in 1966 to encourage blacks to see themselves as a power bloc. At the same time that black power buoyed the hopes of black nationalists, however, it terrified many whites, who viewed it as combative and antiwhite.

In the following article, which originally appeared in a 1966 SNCC publication, Carmichael endorses a black power program to liberate blacks from political, cultural, and economic oppression. To this end, Carmichael exhorts blacks—heretofore dependent on the dominant white society—to return to the ghetto to organize and control their own communities.

In 1967 Carmichael left the SNCC, which had significantly hardened its stance on racial matters under his leadership, to

Stokely Carmichael, "Toward Black Liberation," *The Massachusetts Review*, Autumn 1966.

join the Black Panthers. Shortly after, he moved to Guinea, Africa, and adopted the name Kwame Ture to reflect his African roots.

One of the most pointed illustrations of the need for Black Power, as a positive and redemptive force in a society degenerating into a form of totalitarianism, is to be made by examining the history of distortion that the concept has received in national media of publicity. In this "debate," as in everything else that affects our lives, Negroes are dependent on, and at the discretion of, forces and institutions within the white society which have little interest in representing us honestly. Our experience with the national press has been that where they have managed to escape a meretricious special interest in "Git Whitey" sensationalism and race-war mongering, individual reporters and commentators have been conditioned by the enveloping racism of the society to the point where they are incapable even of objective observation and reporting of racial *incidents*, much less the analysis of *ideas*. But this limitation of vision and perceptions is an inevitable consequence of the dictatorship of definition, interpretation and consciousness, along with the censorship of history that the society has inflicted upon the Negro—and itself.

Our concern for black power addresses itself directly to this problem, the necessity to reclaim our history and our identity from the cultural terrorism and depredation of self-justifying white guilt.

To do this we shall have to struggle for the right to create our own terms through which to define ourselves and our relationship to the society, and to have these terms recognized. This is the first necessity of a free people, and the first right that any oppressor must suspend. The white fathers of American racism knew this—instinctively it seems—as is indicated by the continuous record of the distortion and omission in their dealings with the red and black men. In the same way that southern apologists for the "Jim Crow" society have so obscured, muddied and misrepresented the record of the reconstruction period, until it is almost impossible to tell what really happened, their contemporary counterparts are busy doing the same thing with the recent history of the civil rights movement.

In 1964, for example, the National Democratic Party, led by L. B. Johnson and Hubert H. Humphrey, cynically undermined the efforts of Mississippi's Black population to achieve some degree of political representation. Yet, whenever the events of that convention are recalled by the press, one sees only that version fabricated by the press agents of the Democratic Party. A year later the House of Representatives in an even more vulgar display of political racism made a mockery of the political rights of Mississippi's Negroes when it failed to unseat the Mississippi Delegation to the House which had been elected through a process which methodically and systematically excluded over 450,000 voting-age Negroes, almost one half of the total electorate of the state. Whenever this event is mentioned in print it is in terms which leaves one with the rather curious impression that somehow the oppressed Negro people of Mississippi are at fault for confronting the Congress with a situation in which they had no alternative but to endorse Mississippi's racist political practices.

I mention these two examples because, having been directly involved in them, I can see very clearly the discrepancies between what happened, and the versions that are finding their way into general acceptance as a kind of popular mythology. Thus the victimization of the Negro takes place in two phases—first it occurs in fact and deed, then, and this is equally sinister, in the official recording of those facts.

The "Black Power" program and concept which is being articulated by SNCC, CORE, and a host of community organizations in the ghettoes of the North and South has not escaped that process. The white press had been busy articulating their own analyses, their own interpretations, and criticisms of their own creations. For example, while the press had given wide and sensational dissemination to attacks made by figures in the Civil Rights movement—foremost among which are Roy Wilkins of the NAACP [National Association for the Advancement of Colored People] and Whitney Young of the Urban League—and to the hysterical ranting about black racism made by the political chameleon that now serves as Vice-President, it has generally failed to give accounts of the reasonable and productive dialogue which is taking place in the Negro community, and in certain important areas in the white religious and intellectual community. A national committee of influential Negro Churchmen affiliated with the National Council of Churches, despite their obvious respectability and responsibility, had to resort to a paid advertisement to articulate their position, while anyone shouting the hysterical yappings of "Black Racism" got ample space. Thus the American people have gotten at best a superficial and misleading account of the very terms and tenor of this debate. . . .

Traditionally, for each new ethnic group, the route to social and political integration into America's pluralistic society, has been through the organization of their own institutions with which to represent their communal needs within the larger society. This is simply stating what the advocates of black power are saying. The strident outcry, *particularly* from the liberal community, that has been evoked by this proposal can only be understood by examining the historic relationship between Negro and White power in this country.

Blackness and Powerlessness

Negroes are defined by two forces, their blackness and their powerlessness. There have been traditionally two communities in America. The White community, which controlled and defined the forms that all institutions within the society would take, and the Negro community which has been excluded from participation in the power decisions that shaped the society, and has traditionally been dependent upon, and subservient to the White community.

This has not been accidental. The history of every institution of this society indicates that a major concern in the ordering and structuring of the society has been the maintaining of the Negro community in its condition of dependence and oppression. This has not been on the level of individual acts of discrimination between individual whites against individual Negroes, but as total acts by the White community against the Negro community. This fact cannot be too strongly emphasized—that racist assumptions of white superiority have been so deeply ingrained in the structure of the society that it infuses its entire functioning, and is so much a part of the national subconscious that it is taken for granted and is frequently not even recognized.

Let me give an example of the difference between individual racism and institutionalized racism, and the society's response to both. When unidentified white terrorists bomb a Negro Church and kill five children, that is an act of individual racism, widely deplored by most segments of the society. But when in that same city, Birmingham, Alabama, not five but 500 Negro babies die each year because of a lack of proper food, shelter and medical facilities, and thousands more are destroyed and maimed physically, emotionally and intellectually because of conditions of poverty and deprivation in the ghetto, that is a function of institutionalized racism. But the society either pretends it doesn't know of this situation, or is incapable of doing anything meaningful about it. And this resistance to doing anything meaningful about conditions in that ghetto comes from the fact that the ghetto is itself a product of a combination of forces and special interests in the white community, and the groups that have access to the resources and power to change that situation benefit, politically and economically, from the existence of that ghetto.

It is more than a figure of speech to say that the Negro community in America is the victim of white imperialism and colonial exploitation. This is in practical economic and political terms true. There are over 20 million black people comprising ten percent of this nation. They for the most part live in well-defined areas of the country—in the shanty-towns and rural black belt areas of the South, and increasingly in the slums of northern and western industrial cities. If one goes into any Negro community, whether it be in Jackson, Miss., Cambridge, Md. or Harlem, N.Y., one will find that the same combination of political, economic, and social forces are at work. The people in the Negro community do not control the resources of that community, its political decisions, its law enforcement, its housing standards; and even the physical ownership of the land, houses, and stores *lie outside that community*.

White Power

It is white power that makes the laws, and it is violent white power in the form of armed white cops that enforces those laws with guns and nightsticks. The vast majority of Negroes in this country live in these captive communities and must endure these conditions of oppression because, and only because, *they are black and powerless.* I do not suppose that at any point the men who control the power and resources of this country ever sat down and designed these black enclaves, and formally articulated the terms of their colonial and dependent status, as was done, for example, by the Apartheid government of South Africa. Yet, one can not distinguish between one ghetto and another. As one moves from city to city it is as though some malignant racist planning-unit had done precisely this—designed each one from the same master blueprint. And indeed, if the ghetto had been formally and deliberately planned, instead of growing spontaneously and inevitably from the racist functioning of the various institutions that combine to make the society, it would be somehow less frightening. The situation would be less frightening because, if these ghettoes were the result of design and conspiracy, one could understand their similarity as being artificial and consciously imposed, rather than the result of identical patterns of white racism which repeat themselves in cities as distant as Boston and Birmingham. Without bothering to list the historic factors which contribute to this pattern—economic exploitation, political impotence, discrimination in employment and education—one can see that to correct this pattern will require far-reaching changes in the basic power-relationships and the ingrained social patterns within the society. The question is, of course, what kinds of changes are necessary, and how is it possible to bring them about?

In recent years the answer to these questions which has been given by most articulate groups of Negroes and their white allies, the "liberals" of all stripes, has been in terms of something called "integration." According to the advocates of integration, social justice will be accomplished by "integrating the Negro into the mainstream institutions of the society from which he has been traditionally excluded." It is very significant that each time I have heard this formulation it has been in terms of "the Negro," the individual Negro, rather than in terms of the community.

This concept of integration had to be based on the assumption that there was nothing of value in the Negro community and that little of value could be created among Negroes, so the thing to do was to siphon off the "acceptable" Negroes into the surrounding middle-class white community. Thus the goal of the movement for integration was simply to loosen up the restrictions barring the entry of Negroes into the white community. Goals around which the struggle took place, such as public accommodation, open housing, job opportunity on the executive level (which is easier to deal with than the problem of semi-skilled and blue collar jobs which involve more far-reaching economic adjustments), are quite simply middle-class goals, articulated by a tiny group of Negroes who had middle-class aspirations. It is true that the student demonstrations in the South during the early sixties, out of which SNCC came, had a similar orientation. But while it is hardly a concern of a black sharecropper, dishwasher, or welfare recipient whether a certain fifteen-dollar-a-day motel offers accommodations to Negroes, the overt symbols of white superiority and the imposed limitations on the Negro community had to be destroyed. Now, black people must look beyond these goals, to the issue of collective power.

Such a limited class orientation was reflected not only in the program and goals of the civil rights movement, but in its tactics and organization. It is very significant that the two oldest and most "respectable" civil rights organizations have constitutions which *specifically* prohibit partisan political activity. CORE once did, but changed that clause when it changed its orientation toward black power. But this is perfectly understandable in terms of the strategy and goals of the older organizations. The civil rights movement saw its role as a kind of liaison between the powerful white community and the dependent Negro one. The dependent status of the black community apparently was unimportant since—if the movement were successful—it was going to blend into the white community anyway. We made no pretense of organizing and developing institutions of community power in the Negro community, but appealed to the conscience of white institutions of power. The posture of the civil rights movement was that of the dependent, the suppliant. The theory was that without attempting to create any organized base of political strength itself, the civil rights movement could, by forming coalitions with var-

ious "liberal" pressure organizations in the white community—
liberal reform clubs, labor unions, church groups, progressive
civic groups—and at times one or other of the major political parties—influence national legislation and national social patterns.

A United Program

I think we all have seen the limitations of this approach. We have
repeatedly seen that political alliances based on appeals to conscience and decency are chancy things, simply because institutions
and political organizations have no consciences outside their own
special interests. The political and social rights of Negroes have
been and always will be negotiable and expendable the moment
they conflict with the interests of our "allies." If we do not learn
from history, we are doomed to repeat it, and that is precisely the
lesson of the Reconstruction. Black people were allowed to register, vote and participate in politics because it was to the advantage
of powerful white allies to promote this. But this was the result of
white decision, and it was ended by other white men's decision
before any political base powerful enough to challenge that decision could be established in the southern Negro community.
(Thus at this point in the struggle Negroes have no assurance—
save a kind of idiot optimism and faith in a society whose history
is one of racism—that if it were to become necessary, even the
painfully limited gains thrown to the civil rights movement by the
Congress will not be revoked as soon as a shift in political senti-
ments should occur.)

The major limitation of this approach was that it tended to
maintain the traditional dependence of Negroes, and of the movement. We depended upon the good-will and support of various
groups within the white community whose interests were not always compatible with ours. To the extent that we depended on
the financial support of other groups, we were vulnerable to their
influence and domination.

Also the program that evolved out of this coalition was really
limited and inadequate in the long term and one which affected
only a small select group of Negroes. Its goal was to make the
white community accessible to "qualified" Negroes and presum-
ably each year a few more Negroes armed with their passport—a

couple of university degrees—would escape into middle-class America and adopt the attitudes and life styles of that group; and one day the Harlems and the Watts would stand empty, a tribute to the success of integration. This is simply neither realistic nor particularly desirable. You can integrate communities, but you assimilate individuals. Even if such a program were possible its result would be, not to develop the black community as a functional and honorable segment of the total society, with its own cultural identity, life patterns, and institutions, but to abolish it—the final solution to the Negro problem. Marx said that the working class is the first class in history that ever wanted to abolish itself. If one listens to some of our "moderate" Negro leaders it appears that the American Negro is the first race that ever wished to abolish itself. The fact is that what must be abolished is not the black community, but the dependent colonial status that has been inflicted upon it. The racial and cultural personality of the black community must be preserved and the community must win its freedom while preserving its cultural integrity. This is the essential difference between integration as it is currently practiced and the concept of black power.

What has the movement for integration accomplished to date? The Negro graduating from M.I.T. with a doctorate will have better job opportunities available to him than to Lynda Bird Johnson. But the rate of unemployment in the Negro community is steadily increasing, while that in the white community decreases. More educated Negroes hold executive jobs in major corporations and federal agencies than ever before, but the gap between white income and Negro income has almost doubled in the last twenty years. More suburban housing is available to Negroes, but housing conditions in the ghetto are steadily declining. While the infant mortality rate of New York City is at its lowest rate ever in the city's history, the infant mortality rate of Harlem is steadily climbing. There has been an organized national resistance to the Supreme Court's order to integrate the schools, and the federal government has not acted to enforce that order. Less than fifteen percent of black children in the South attend integrated schools; and Negro schools, which the vast majority of black children still attend, are increasingly decrepit, over-crowded, under-staffed, inadequately equipped and funded. This explains why the rate of school dropouts is increasing among Negro teenagers, who then express their bitterness, hopelessness, and alienation by the only means they have—rebellion. As long as people in the ghettoes of our large cities feel that they are victims of the misuse of white power without any way to have their needs represented—and these are frequently simple needs: to get the welfare inspectors to stop kicking down your doors in the middle of the night, the cops from beating your children, the landlord to exterminate the vermin in your home, the city to collect your garbage—we will continue to have riots. These are not the products of "black power," but of the absence of any organization capable of giving the community the power, the black power, to deal with its problems.

SNCC proposes that it is now time for the black freedom movement to stop pandering to the fears and anxieties of the white middle class in the attempt to earn its "good-will," and to return to the ghetto to organize these communities to control themselves. This organization must be attempted in northern and southern urban areas as well as in the rural black belt counties of the South. The chief antagonist to this organization is, in the South, the overtly racist Democratic party, and in the North the equally corrupt big city machines.

The standard argument presented against independent political organization is "But you are only 10%." I cannot see the relevance of this observation, since no one is talking about taking over the country, but taking control over our own communities.

The fact is that the Negro population, 10% or not, is very strategically placed because—ironically—of segregation. What is also true is that Negroes have never been able to utilize the full voting potential of our numbers. Where we could vote, the case has always been that the white political machine stacks and gerrymanders the political subdivision in Negro neighborhoods so the true voting strength is never reflected in political strength. Would anyone looking at the distribution of political power in Manhattan, ever think that Negroes represented 60% of the population there?

Just as often the effective political organization in Negro communities is absorbed by tokenism and patronage—the time honored practice of "giving" certain offices to selected Negroes. The machine thus creates a "little machine," which is subordinate and responsive to it, in the Negro community. These Negro political "leaders" are really vote deliverers, more responsible to the white machine and the white power structure, than to the community they allegedly represent. Thus the white community is able to substitute patronage control for audacious black power in the Negro community. This is precisely what Johnson tried to do even before the Voting Rights Act of 1966 was passed. The National Democrats made it very clear that the measure was intended to register Democrats, not Negroes. The President and top officials of the Democratic Party called in almost 100 selected Negro "leaders" from the Deep South. Nothing was said about changing the policies of the racist state parties, nothing was said about repudiating such leadership figures as [James] Eastland and Ross Barnett in Mississippi or George Wallace in Alabama. What was said was simply "Go home and organize your people into the local Democratic Party—*then* we'll see about poverty money and appointments." (Incidentally, for the most part the War on Poverty in the South is controlled by local Democratic ward heelers—and outspoken racists who have used the program to change the form of the Negroes' dependence. People who were afraid to register for fear of being thrown off the farm are now afraid to register for fear of losing their Head-Start jobs.)

Black Community Power

We must organize black community power to end these abuses, and to give the Negro community a chance to have its needs expressed. A leadership which is truly "responsible"—not to the white press and power structure, but to the community—must be developed. Such leadership will recognize that its power lies in the unified and collective strength of that community. This will make it difficult for the white leadership group to conduct its dialogue with individuals in terms of patronage and prestige, and will force them to talk to the community's representatives in terms of real power.

The single aspect of the black power program that has encountered most criticism is this concept of independent organization. This is presented as third-partyism which has never worked, or a withdrawal into black nationalism and isolationism. If such a program is developed it will not have the effect of isolating the Negro community but the reverse. When the Negro community is able to control local office, and negotiate with other groups from a position of organized strength, the possibility of meaningful political alliances on specific issues will be increased. That is a rule of politics and there is no reason why it should not operate here. The only difference is that we will have the power to define the terms of these alliances.

The next question usually is, "So—can it work, can the ghettoes in fact be organized?" The answer is that this organization must be successful, because there are no viable alternatives—not the War on Poverty, which was at its inception limited to dealing with effects rather than causes, and has become simply another source of machine patronage. And "Integration" is meaningful only to a small chosen class within the community.

The revolution in agricultural technology in the South is displacing the rural Negro community into northern urban areas. Both Washington, D.C. and Newark, N.J. have Negro majorities. One third of Philadelphia's population of two million people is black. "Inner city" in most major urban areas is already predominantly Negro, and with the white rush to suburbia, Negroes will in the next three decades control the heart of our great cities. These areas can become either concentration camps with a bitter and volatile population whose only power is the power to destroy, or organized and powerful communities able to make constructive contributions to the total society. Without the power to control their lives and their communities, without effective political institutions through which to relate to the total society, these communities will exist in a constant state of insurrection. This is a choice that the country will have to make.

Viewpoint 6

"'Black Power' is a bitter retreat from the possibility of the attainment of the goals of any serious racial integration in America."

Black Power Is Ineffective

Kenneth Clark

The noted psychologist Kenneth Clark is most often remembered for his contribution to the NAACP brief that led to the historic 1954 ruling by the U.S. Supreme Court in *Brown v. Board of Education* that outlawed school segregation. In the following address delivered in October 1967 before the convention of the Association for the Study of Negro Life and History, Clark addresses the failed promises of the civil rights revolution—and the subsequent rise of black power. In his analysis, Clark concedes that black power does indeed exert a tremendous psychological boost to frustrated and disillusioned blacks. In the end, however, black power is pragmatically futile, as it tends to subjugate rational thought and planning to "dogmatism and fanaticism." Instead, blacks must find implementable solutions to the overwhelming racial problems that continue to plague American society.

Kenneth Clark, "The Present Dilemma of the Negro," *Journal of Negro History*, vol. LIII, January 1968, pp. 1–11. Copyright © 1968 by The Association for the Study of African-American Life and History. Reproduced by permission.

The "nuclear" irony of American history and the American social, political, and economic system is that the destiny of the enslaved and disadvantaged Negro determines the destiny of the nation. The fundamental fact around which all questions of national survival pivot is the fact of inherent racial inter-relatedness—or integration, if you please—in spite of the persistent demands and attempts to impose racial separatism. The problems of the American Negro are problems of America. The conflicts, aspirations, confusions, and doubts of Negro Americans are not merely similar but are identical to those of white Americans. The Negro need not yearn to be assimilated into American culture—he is and determines American culture. In the face of rapid and at times frightening historical, economic, political, technological, social, and intellectual changes, the Negro remains the constant, and at times irritating reality that is America. He remains the essential psychological reality with which America must continuously seek to come to terms—and in so doing is formed by.

The moral and ethical aspirations of America have been accepted totally by Negroes. The moral schizophrenia of America is reflected most clearly in the status of Negroes, starting with slavery and continuing to the contemporary ghettoes which blight the powerful and affluent cities of our nation.

American Racism

The dilemmas of America are the dilemmas of Negro Americans. One cannot, therefore, discuss the dilemmas of the contemporary American Negro without at the same time becoming involved in an analysis of the historical and psychological fabric of American life. This is the thesis reflecting the bias of a social psychologist—a bias which might be rejected by more sophisticated historians, political and economic theorists, or tougher minded social critics. I nonetheless base my thesis on the psychological premise that the values, attitudes, and behavior of individual human beings and groups of human beings are determined by the complex socialization process—that normal human beings are modifiable and are determined by their environment and culture—and not by any inherent, genetic or racial determinants.

Let us now be specific:

A basic dilemma of America is whether the Negro should be accepted and taken seriously as a human being and permitted the rights and privileges accorded other human beings in our political system. America has endured slave rebellions, developed an underground railroad, fought one of the most bloody wars in human history and is now undergoing a series of urban ghetto implosions in the attempt to resolve this persistent bedeviling question.

The Negro's form of this basic dilemma is whether to persist in his insistence upon his unqualified rights as a human being without regard to the risks or consequences—or whether to accommodate to the resistances by subtle or flagrant forms of withdrawal from the fray. The general acceptance of slavery, the many psychological adjustments and deflection of aggressive reactions to subjugation, the varieties of back-to-Africa movements, the cults, fads, and the recent series of riots in our ghettos are among the many ways in which American Negroes have sought to deal with this basic American dilemma.

The gnawing doubts of white Americans as to their status and worth as human beings—the deep feelings of inferiority coming out of the actual inferior status in the land of their origin in Europe—impelled American whites to develop and enforce social and institutional arrangements designed to inflict upon Negroes an inferior status in American life. This was necessary to bolster the demanding status needs of whites. These needs were powerful enough to counteract the logic, the morality and the powerful political ethics of the egalitarian and democratic rhetoric which is also an important American reality. . . . American democratic creed and ideals are not psychologically contradictory to American racism. In terms of dynamics and motivation of the insecure, they are compatible.

The Dilemma of Black Americans

This critical American dilemma is reflectcd in Negroes not only in terms of acceptance of the creeds and its promises literally, but also in terms of deep doubts concerning the worth of self. The former aspect of the dilemma stems from the fact of general indoctrination which transcends even the barriers of racially segregated schools and is reinforced by the development of the mass media in the 20th century. The latter component of the Negro's dilemma arises out of the reality of the inferior status to which he has been subjugated. The walls of segregation are not only humiliating—but given this type of chronic humiliation there develops self doubt, subtle and flagrant forms of self hatred, personal and group frustrations, internalized hostility, aggressions, self denial or bombast. Under these conditions the walls of segregation become pathetically protective. Within them the subjugated individuals need not meet the tests of free and open competition—need not expose vulnerable egos to single standards of competence.

The anguish and resistance of anxious, self-doubting white segregationists and the cautious timidity of striving middle class whites with the psyche of affluent peasants are matched only by the anxieties, doubts, and vacillation of vast numbers of Negroes—working and middle class—as they stand at the threshold of non-segregated society and are confronted by the tremendous psychological challenges for which American history not only did not prepare them but erected seemingly insurmountable barriers. The demand for racial justice on the part of the American Negroes is balanced by an almost equal psychological reality of the fear of the removal of racial barriers.

Within this context—disturbing and painful, but I believe psychologically valid—one can now attempt an analysis of the contemporary manifestations of the dilemma of America and the dilemma of Negro Americans. The value of such an analysis will be determined by whether it provides a basis for constructive, realistic, democratic, and humane resolutions of some of the racial and social problems which afflict America and threaten its survival.

In many disturbing ways the problems of race relations in America today are similar to those of the post-Reconstruction period of the late 19th century which continued and intensified through World War I. This period, which Rayford Logan and John Hope Franklin have described as the "nadir" of the Negro in American life, came as a seemingly abrupt and certainly cruel repudiation of the promises of Reconstruction for inclusion of the Negro into the political and economic life of the nation. This was a period:

—when the white crusaders for racial justice and democracy became weary as the newly freed Negroes could no longer be considered a purely Southern problem;

—when the aspirations for and movement of Negroes toward justice and equality were curtailed and reversed by organized violence and barbarity perpetrated against them;

—when, as a result of their abandonment and powerlessness, the frustrations, bitterness and despair of Negroes increased and displaced optimism and hope.

This period culminated in the institutionalization of rigid forms of racism—the enactment and enforcement of laws requiring or permitting racial discrimination and segregation in all aspects of American life. This retrogression in racial democracy, in America was imposed by white segregationists with the apathy, indifference, or quiet acceptance of white liberals and moderates as necessary accessories.

The parallel with the state of race relations in America today is stark and frightening. The promises and optimism of the Second Reconstruction, initiated by the pattern of litigation which resulted in the *Brown* decision of 1954—which precipitated the high morale mark of the successful boycotts and sit-ins, and which reached its climax in the emotional catharsis of the 1963 March on Washington—were also cruelly aborted by stepped-up violence against Negro and white civil rights workers in the resistant Southern states and the related weariness, racial anxieties, and latent racism of Northern whites which emerged under the guise of "white backlash."

"Black Power"

The hopes and beliefs of the Negro that racial equality and democracy could be obtained through litigation, legislation, executive action, and negotiation, and though strong alliances with various white liberal groups, were supplanted by disillusionment, bitterness, and anger which erupted under the anguished cry of "Black Power" which pathetically sought to disguise the understandable desperation and impotence with bombast and rhetoric.

A critical danger—and probably a difference without a pragmatic distinction—between the determinants of retrogression in the first post-Reconstruction period and the present is that whereas the promises of racial progress were reversed in the 19th century by the fanaticism, irrationality, and cruel strength of white segregationists—the impending racial retrogression of today might come about largely through self-hatred leading to the fanaticism, dogmatism, rigidity, and self-destructive cruelty of black separatists. If this comes about, it will not be enough to excuse this monstrous perpetuation of the lie of racism and postponement of the goals of democracy and humanity by asserting that the frustrations and bitterness of the victimized Negro account for his present irrationality and rigidity. A similar and equally valid psychological explanation could be offered to explain the racial cruelties of desperate and miserable poor whites of the past and present. Understanding is not acceptance.

White segregationists were able to inflict and perpetuate racial injustices upon Negroes because rational, sophisticated, and moderate whites were silent in the face of barbarities. They permitted themselves to be intimidated and bullied by white extremists until they were morally and almost functionally indistinguishable from their worst and most ignorant elements. A similar threat and dilemma face the rational, thoughtful Negro today. If he permits himself to be cowed into silence by unrealistic Negro racists, he will be an active partner in fastening the yoke of impossible racial separatism more tightly around the neck of America. He—you, through your silence, will permit the difficult goals of a racially nonsegregated society to be lost by default. You would have given to black racists what you, your fathers and grandfathers fought and died to prevent giving to white racists. The victories which white segregationists, in spite of all their material and political power, could not have won for themselves, black separatists would have won for them—and we through our silence would make this possible.

To prevent the repetition of the tragedy of racial retrogression and a return to the "nadir" of race relations in America, we must be realistic in our appraisal of the present state of race relations in America. . . . We must analyze as tough-mindedly as possible the dynamics and symptoms of our times if we are to develop effective and realistic remedies.

During the past few years it became excruciatingly clear for the Negro that the more things changed the more they remained the same—or worsened. The promises and hope for progress became a relentless quagmire of words.

The drama of direct action, non-violent confrontation of the more obvious signs of Southern racial injustice became trite, and was not particularly relevant or effective in dealing with the persistent, pervasive, and subtle problems of racism which afflicted the Northern Negro. More appropriate and effective methods have not yet been found to deal with Northern racism.

The guilt and indignation of some Northern whites against Southern forms of racism turned into white backlash or mutism when the Northern Negro began to take seriously the claims of civil rights progress and sought some observable signs of them in Northern cities.

The anguish and desperation of the Northern Negro have been expressed in the latest series of ghetto eruptions which started in the Harlem riot of the summer of 1964, reached a crescendo in the Watts riot of 1965 and continued through the current series of riots in Newark and Detroit of this past summer. Another significant expression of the Northern Negro's "no-win" fatalism is found in the rise of the "Black Power" slogan and momentum which skyrocketed at the time of the Meredith shooting in Mississippi in June of 1966 and continues as an obbligato to the sounds of ghetto violence and futility.

"Black Power" and "White Backlash"

It is important to keep in mind the date (June, 1966) when the "Black Power" slogan became nationally advertised—in order not to be confused about the cause and effect relationship between "Black Power" and "white backlash."

Whatever may be its tactical, strategic, and rational shortcomings and its ambiguity, "Black Power" did not cause "white backlash" . . . The existence of "white backlash," the unwillingness of whites to be serious in meeting the demands of Negroes for the same rights and responsibilities granted as a matter of course to all other Americans—including the newest refugee from European, Latin American, or Asiatic oppression—caused the outbursts of hysterical bitterness and random hostility inherent in the cry of "Black Power."

"Black Power" emerged as a response to the following facts:

—a recognition of the fact that the center of gravity of the civil rights movement had moved to the Northern urban racial ghettos where it was now immobilized by ambiguous intensified white resistance to any meaningful change in the predicament of Negroes;

—the recognition of the fact that successful litigation, strong legislation, free access to public accommodations, open housing laws, strong pronouncements on the part of the President, governors or mayors, and even the right to vote or to hold office were not relevant to the overriding fact that the masses of Negroes were still confined to poverty and to the dehumanizing conditions of the ghetto;

—and that in spite of the promises of a Great Society and the activity of the war on poverty, the Negro's children were still doomed to criminally inferior schools and his youth and males the victims of unemployment, underemployment and stagnation.

"Black Power" is the cry of defiance of what its advocates have come to see as the hoax of racial progress—of the cynicism of the appeals to the Negro to be patient and to be lawful as his needs are continually subordinated to more important national and international issues and to the needs, desires, and conveniences of more privileged groups.

Whites, by virtue of their numerical, military, and economic superiority, reinforced by historical American racism which grants higher status to whites by virtues of skin color alone, do have the power to decide whether the future of Negroes—the Negro masses, the Negro middle class, or the Negro elected official—will be positive, negative, or stagnant.

This core reality of the dynamics of power is not likely to be influenced by sentimental and idealistic appeals for justice, by smiles or promises or by emotional sloganeering.

The Psychological Appeal of "Black Power"

"Black Power," in spite of its ambiguity, its "no-win" premise, its programmatic emptiness and its pragmatic futility does have tremendous psychological appeal for the masses of Negroes who have "nothing to lose" and stone middle class Negroes who are revolted by the empty promises and the moral dry-rot of affluent America.

"Black Power" is a bitter retreat from the possibility of the attainment of the goals of any serious racial integration in America. . . .

It is an attempt to make a verbal virtue of involuntary racial segregation. . . .

It is the sour grapes phenomenon on the American racial scene. . . .

"Black Power" is the contemporary form of the Booker T. Washington accommodation to white America's resistance to making democracy real for Negro Americans. While Booker T. made his adjustment to and acceptance of white racism under the guise of conservatism, many if not all of the "Black Power" advocates are seeking to sell the same shoddy moral product in the gaudy package of racial militance.

Nonetheless, today "Black Power" is a reality in the Negro ghettos of America—increasing in emotional intensity, if not in rational clarity. And we, if we are to be realistic, cannot afford to pretend that it does not exist. Even in its most irrational and illusory formulations—and particularly when it is presented as a vague and incoherent basis upon which the deprived Negro can project his own pathetic wishes for a pride and an assertiveness which white America continues mockingly or piously to deny him—"Black Power" is a powerful political reality which cannot be ignored by realistic Negro or white political officials.

It is all too clear that among the casualties of the present phase of American race relations are reason, clarity, consistency and realism. Some "Black Power" spokesmen, like their white segregationist counterparts, demand the subjugation of rational and realistic thought and planning to dogmaticism and fanaticism. By their threats and name calling, they seek to intimidate others into silence or a mindless mouthing of their slogans.

To be effective and to increase his chances of survival in the face of name-calling verbal racial militants, the trained Negro must demonstrate that he is concerned and can bring about some positive changes in the following intolerable areas of ghetto life:

1. criminally inefficient and racially segregated public schools;
2. dehumanizingly poor housing;
3. pervasive job discrimination and joblessness;
4. shoddy quality of goods and high prices in local stores;
5. the dirt, filth, and stultifying drabness of ghetto streets and neighborhoods;
6. the adversary relationship between police and the residents of the ghettos.

This requires the mobilization and use of human intelligence to define the problems, to study and analyze them and to develop practical and implementable solutions to them. This cannot be done on the basis of race—whites and Negroes must join together in an experiment to determine whether systematic and emphatic use of human intelligence and training can be a form of power which can be used constructively in the quest for solutions of long standing urban and racial problems. This is the rationale of The Metropolitan Applied Research Center. We are under no illusions that this will be easy. . . . We know that power confrontation brings risks not found in the cloistered halls of academia. We know that we cannot expect the protections and safety of the detached isolated scholars. But we believe that human intelligence is a social trust and that the stakes are worth the risks.

Viewpoint 7

"King's nonviolent tactics could not have destroyed the South's racial system."

King's Protest Campaigns Had a Limited Impact on Civil Rights

Denton L. Watson

Denton L. Watson charges that Martin Luther King Jr. and his nonviolent direct action campaign played a limited role in the civil rights movement. In truth, the NAACP was the real vanguard of the movement. Watson uses the Montgomery bus boycott as a case in point: Although it publicized black demands, the boycott would not have been successful without the legal backing of the NAACP. Indeed, throughout the pivotal years of the civil rights movement, the NAACP created meaningful legislation and protected the constitutional rights of blacks, which, in turn, profoundly altered the social, economic, and political conditions that affected African Americans. Watson is the author of *Lion in the Lobby: Clarence Mitchell Jr.'s Struggle for the*

Denton L. Watson, "Did King Scholars Skew Our Views of Civil Rights?" *The Chronicle of Higher Education*, vol. 37, January 23, 1991, p. A44. Copyright © 1991 by *The Chronicle of Higher Education*. This article may not be published, reposted, or redistributed without express permission from *The Chronicle*. Reproduced by permission of the author.

Passage of Civil Rights Laws. He contributed the following article
to the *Chronicle of Higher Education.*

Given the extent to which scholars have rewritten history by
making Martin Luther King, Jr., the pivotal figure in the civil
rights struggle, few of those now criticizing him for plagiarism are
qualified to cast the first stone. His admirers have built him up to
the point where it is easy to knock him down. Scholars have not
looked objectively at his whole personality and have credited him
with accomplishments of others; they must recognize that King's
strategies had serious weaknesses, his aura of greatness was wan-
ing later in the movement, and his assassination contributed
greatly to his stature.

The Front Lines

Among others, people who worked with the Student Nonviolent
Coordinating Committee (SNCC) and the Congress of Racial
Equality (CORE) say King wasn't the only leader confronting
racial oppression in the South. They, too, were on the front lines.
During the struggle, the consensus was that the now-almost-
forgotten Roy Wilkins and the National Association for the Advancement of Colored People (NAACP) that he headed were the
vanguard of the movement.

And A. Philip Randolph, head of the Brotherhood of Sleeping
Car Porters, was the acknowledged "dean" of the movement.
From well before he got Franklin Roosevelt to create the Fair Employment Practice Committee in 1941, he was a driving force for
black equality. The FEPC begins the modern civil rights movement; it is the first time a U.S. President acted to directly prohibit
racial discrimination.

Further, it was Clarence Mitchell, Jr., head of the NAACP
Washington Bureau, who led the struggle to pass civil rights
laws—the movement's primary goal after the U.S. Supreme
Court's 1954 decision in *Brown v. Board of Education* outlawing
school segregation. Scholars have not paid enough attention to
the NAACP and its leaders or understood basic differences between King's goals and the organization's. The struggle's basic

thrusts were constitutional and political, despite King's emphasis on appeals to morality. King's nonviolent tactics could not have destroyed the South's racial system. It was the NAACP that breathed new life into the Fourteenth and Fifteenth Amendments through the courts and executed legislative strategies that led to passage in 1957 of the first civil rights law in 82 years, paving the way for all subsequent legislation of the period.

King's Weaknesses

No one was more aware than King of his own weaknesses or of the differences between his strategies and those of the NAACP. King saw the struggle as a "three-lane road with some emphasizing the way of litigation and mobilizing forces for meaningful legislation, and others emphasizing the way of nonviolent direct action, and still others [like the National Urban League] moving through research and education and building up forces to prepare the Negro for the challenges of a highly industrialized society."

The nonviolent direct action King was advocating, he explained, "does not minimize works through the courts. But it recognizes that legislation and court orders can only declare rights; they can never thoroughly deliver them. Only when the people themselves begin to act are rights on paper given life blood. A catalyst is needed to breathe life experiences into a judicial decision by the persistent exercise of the rights until they become usual and ordinary in human conduct."

Mitchell, NAACP chief strategist, agreed. But he knew that the laws first had to be enacted and that the courts had to uphold them.

King was very human and quietly but intensely competitive. Had scholars properly examined that, they would not have been so shocked over charges of plagiarism. King tended to invade areas where CORE and SNCC had established bases. This often led young activists in those groups to speak disparagingly of him as "de lawd" and to challenge his focus on arousing the national conscience, in contrast to goals such as voter-registration programs, for example.

The Montgomery, Alabama, bus boycott King led was an enduring display of the dominance of the human spirit, but there are real limits to human endurance, as evident from increasing discouragement among boycotters shortly before the NAACP won a ruling from the U.S. Supreme Court that segregation on city buses was unconstitutional. Had the NAACP not stepped in, the boycott would have failed. Yet, King downplayed the extent to which the success of the bus boycott depended on NAACP legal machinery, and scholars have followed suit.

King's egotistical weakness is also seen in his book, *Why We Can't Wait*, when he claimed that the "Negro Revolution" had "struck" in 1963, that "nonviolent direct action proved that it would win victories without losing wars, and so became the triumphant tactic of the Negro Revolution of 1963." In fact, 1963 was the climax of a long awakening African Americans that began in the closing days of the New Deal, not a sudden, explosive testament to King's nonviolent philosophy.

King claimed the bloody demonstrations in Birmingham, Alabama, had forced the Kennedy Administration to place "a strong civil rights bill at the top of the congressional calendar." That was partly true. Cries of nonviolent demonstrators reeling from Police Commissioner Bull Connor's fire hoses, police dogs, and night sticks did pierce the ears of an obtuse Kennedy Administration. But it took another barbarous act to move President Kennedy to ask Congress for the strong civil rights bill needed. The assassination of NAACP Mississippi field secretary Medgar Evers forced the President to move beyond expressing anger at the Birmingham violence.

King's Contribution

King was indeed a catalyst and will always remain a monumental figure in civil rights history. His greatest contribution was his ability to arouse the human spirit to unparalleled heights and to burden the consciences of white liberals. Yet, the nonviolent demonstrations had limited impact on the legislative struggle in Congress, where reason, constitutional concerns, and political weight—not moral appeals or emotionalism—mattered most.

Mitchell said the demonstrations could not have "changed enough minds to do the whole job" and "didn't have the slightest effect" on lawmakers like the Chairman of the House Rules Committee. The legislation got through his committee, Mitchell said, only "because we had the votes to outvote him."

To be fair to King and the civil rights movement, scholars must separate myth from reality through objective historical assessments, doing more comprehensive analyses of the movement from perspectives other than King's. They need to study with equal devotion the legislative thrusts led by Wilkins and Mitchell, as well as contributions of constitutional giants like Charles Hamilton Houston, who established the NAACP legal program; of his protege, Thurgood Marshall; and of many gifted lawyers.

Scholars should demonstrate awareness that the civil rights revolution, though led by blacks with support of while liberals, could have been won only with the help of political conservatives. Mitchell was as much indebted to Republican conservatives as he was to Republican and Democratic civil rights standard bearers.

It was broad-based support of the struggle to protect the constitutional rights of all citizens that made the civil rights revolution the most important period in U.S. history after the American Revolution and the Civil War. It is time scholars began writing a much fuller version of the movement.

Viewpoint 8

"Mass mobilization and local organization did the most to transform the racial landscape of the South."

King's Protest Campaigns Bolstered Civil Rights

Adam Mack

In the following viewpoint, Adam Mack writes that Martin Luther King Jr.'s direct-action and mass mobilization campaigns played a pivotal role in promoting positive racial change during the civil rights movement. Specifically, King's mass protests against Jim Crow—in Birmingham and Selma, for example—drew national attention to the cause of civil rights and compelled the federal government to take decisive action. In contrast, the NAACP's legalistic approach was limited, primarily because many of the legal rulings that pertained to civil rights had little or no impact outside of the courtroom. For example, many southern schools succumbed to massive white resistance and remained segregated even after the Supreme Court mandated desegregation in *Brown v. Board of Education*. Mack is an instructor at the University of South Carolina.

Adam Mack, "The Civil Rights Movement Was More than Just an Accretion of Legal Precedents: It Was a Change in the Hearts and Minds of a People, and It Is Best Understood as a Mass Action," *History in Dispute, Vol. 2: American Social and Political Movements, 1945–2000: Pursuit of Liberty,* edited by Robert J. Allison. Detroit: St. James Press, 2000. Copyright © 2000 by The Gale Group, Inc. Reproduced by permission.

In 1989 veteran activist Bob Moses wrote that the Civil Rights movement was characterized by two distinct organizing traditions. The first was concerned with large-scale community mobilization, generally for national goals, and was represented by familiar events such as the March on Washington and the protests in Birmingham and Selma. The second tradition involved work at the local level, focusing on grassroots organizing and development of indigenous leadership. Representing departures from the legalistic strategy practiced by the National Association for the Advancement of Colored People (NAACP), these two organizing traditions were primarily responsible for the major changes brought by the Civil Rights movement. Community mobilization prompted the federal government to pass transformative civil-rights legislation that dismantled the system of legalized segregation in the South, and grassroots organizing empowered black communities by helping develop leaders and institutions to carry forth the struggle for the long term. The Civil Rights movement was a collaborative effort and legalistic activism made significant contributions to its success, but mass mobilization and local organization did the most to transform the racial landscape of the South.

The Legalistic Approach

There can be no doubt that legalistic activism furthered the civil-rights cause. A key point is that for the first half of the twentieth century racial segregation was entrenched in state law and, since the 1896 *Plessy v. Ferguson* decision, endorsed by the Supreme Court. Victories won by the legal arm of the NAACP from the 1930s through the 1950s—which included judgments against the white primary (1944), segregation in interstate travel (1946), racially restrictive covenants (1948), separate graduate and professional schools for blacks, and eventually segregation in all levels of public education (1954)—thus made critical contributions to the freedom struggle by undermining the legal structure of Jim Crow in the South. At the same time, these victories put the weight of the Constitution behind the emerging Civil Rights movement, giving moral as well as legal credibility to its goals.

Nevertheless, the NAACP's legalistic strategy was a limited instrument for racial change. As much as legal victories seemed to promise the downfall of Jim Crow, court decisions were not self-enforcing; without strong federal support, they could be evaded relatively easily by Southern obstructionists. This situation became painfully obvious in the aftermath of the court victories of the 1940s and 1950s. Although the Supreme Court removed a major obstacle to African American disfranchisement by outlawing the white primary, whites continued to keep blacks from the polls through a combination of intimidation and technical devices such as literacy tests. Moreover, the Court's ruling against segregated interstate travel was ignored in most of the South, and discrimination in housing and employment remained a fact of life. Perhaps the best example of Southern racial intransigence was white resistance to *Brown v. Board of Education of Topeka, Kansas*, the 1954 Supreme Court decision that declared segregation in public schools unconstitutional. Although *Brown* had an immediate effect on school desegregation in parts of the Upper South, it had essentially no impact in the Deep South, as whites mounted a campaign of massive resistance to the ruling. While the NAACP undertook the time-consuming business of filing desegregation suits, obstructionists used violence, token integration plans, and a host of creative legal devices to prevent implementation of the *Brown* decision. Meanwhile, the federal government refused to aggressively enforce the decision, enduring if not promoting Southern defiance.

Only when African Americans mobilized for direct confrontations with the Jim Crow system was the entire federal government compelled to intervene to help make real changes in the South. By the early 1960s, civil-rights proponents had learned that the best way to force the federal government to take decisive action was to create a crisis that drew national attention to the overt denial of basic citizenship rights to African Americans. More than any other civil-rights organization, Martin Luther King Jr.'s Southern Christian Leadership Conference (SCLC) succeeded in mobilizing black communities for dramatic nonviolent protest campaigns that captured media attention, aroused public support, and prompted federal intervention, including the passage of civil-rights legislation.

This strategy was used most effectively in nonviolent direct-action campaigns in Birmingham and Selma, Alabama. Both these campaigns brought the brutality of white supremacy to light by generating shocking scenes of local law enforcement using violence to suppress peaceful demonstrations. Appearing on the front pages of national newspapers and on television, events in Birmingham and Selma led to significant increases in public sympathy for the movement and moved the ever hesitant officials in Washington to take a stronger stand for civil rights. According to Adam Fairclough in *To Redeem the Soul of America: The Southern Christian Leadership Conference and Martin Luther King, Jr.* (1987), the turbulent events of the Birmingham campaign and the spinoff demonstrations that followed convinced the Kennedy administration—which had been following a piecemeal civil-rights policy—that racial crises would continue to occur in the South unless the federal government took action by passing strong civil-rights legislation. This decision, Fairclough argues, led John F. Kennedy to introduce legislation that was eventually passed as the Civil Rights Act of 1964, a measure that expanded the federal government's power to challenge segregation in public accommodations. Two years after the Birmingham protests, SCLC launched a campaign in Selma to address the problem of black disfranchisement, an issue not adequately addressed in the Civil Rights Act. As Fairclough has pointed out, the public reaction to the suppression of demonstrations in Selma energized the Johnson administration's efforts to produce a strong voting-rights law, increased Congressional support for such legislation, and thus paved the way for the Voting Rights Act of 1965.

The 1964–1965 federal civil-rights legislation was not a panacea for problems facing African Americans in the South, but its significance should not be underestimated. Unlike previous Supreme Court decisions and earlier civil-rights laws, the 1964 Civil Rights Act and the 1965 Voting Rights Act included strong enforcement measures and brought dramatic change to the South. Although there was some resistance to the Civil Rights Act, within a relatively short time after its passage, Jim Crow signs came down in much of Dixie, and public accommodations were opened, in a legal sense, to blacks. Described by Fairclough as the "crowning achievement of the civil rights movement," the Voting Rights Act transformed the South's political landscape. By providing new methods of enforcement such as federal registrars and election observers, as well as the suspension of literacy and other voting tests, the act streamlined the government's ability to protect African American voting rights. In the decade after its passage black voter registration increased significantly (in Mississippi it leapt from 6.7 percent to 67.4 percent), more and more African Americans were elected to public office, and unfavorable white candidates were defeated. Although whites continued to hold the lion's share of regional political power, the growth in the black electorate ushered in a new racial tone in southern politics as white politicians openly courted black votes; visible political racism generally became a thing of the past.

However, direct action alone did not engender the transformative civil-rights legislation of the mid 1960s. Indeed, part of the credit must go to NAACP lobbyists who helped push the measures through Congress. Similarly, while the NAACP did not fully embrace direct-action tactics, the protest campaigns of the mid 1960s benefited from timely legal and financial aid from the association. As King and other civil-rights proponents realized, the success of the movement depended on the interplay of NAACP-style legalism and direct action practiced by other groups; scholars should think twice before separating the two approaches completely. As King put it, "Direct action is not a substitute for work in the courts and the halls of government. Bringing about passage of a new and broad law by a city council, state legislature or the Congress, or pleading cases before the courts of the land, does not eliminate the necessity for bringing about the mass dramatization of injustice in front of a city hall. Indeed, direct action and legal action and complement one another; when skillfully employed, each becomes more effective."

Grassroots Efforts

Of course, the movement would not have accomplished anything without local people who took to the streets to challenge Jim Crow. Yet for ordinary African Americans, the gains achieved through direct-action protest went beyond the passage of strong civil-rights legislation. The act of striking a blow for their own freedom—something difficult to do when activism was focused in faraway courtrooms—promoted a new sense of self-determination and self-respect.

Reflecting on the movement in the mid 1970s, Franklin McCain, one of the four black students who started the Greensboro, North Carolina, sit-in movement, described his feelings after participating in his first demonstration: "If it's possible to know what it means to have your soul cleansed—I felt pretty clean at that time. I probably felt better on that day than I've ever felt in my life. Seems like lot of feelings of guilt or what-have-you suddenly left me, and I felt as though I had gained my manhood, so to speak, and not only gained it, but had developed quite a lot of respect for it. Not Franklin McCain only as an individual, but I felt as though the manhood of a number of other black persons had been restored and had gotten some respect from just that one day."

In recent years scholars have looked closely at how the movement changed the lives of local people, turning their attention from the familiar protest campaigns led by King and the SCLC to the less-glamorous work of organizing at the grassroots level. Sustained local organizing, these historians argue, wrought remarkable change by empowering black communities through the cultivation of indigenous leadership and the creation of institutions to support movement activity for the long term. . . .

The Civil Rights movement did not end the problem of race in America. It did, however, destroy the system of legalized segregation that imposed second-class citizenship on African Americans in the South. Equally important, the movement empowered blacks at the local level by helping indigenous leadership and movement-related institutions take root. Only when the focus of reform efforts shifted from a legalistic approach to a strategy based on community mobilization and grassroots organizing did these changes become possible. Court victories and legislative lobbying helped effect change, but the real credit belongs to the activists and ordinary people who confronted Jim Crow in the streets.

CHAPTER 4

Who Played the Most Important Role in the Civil Rights Movement?

✳ Chapter Preface

The civil rights movement of the 1950s and 1960s radically altered the social, political, and economic conditions that affect all minorities in the United States. While the most conspicuous change was the abolishment of restrictions that kept blacks separated from whites, the freedoms gained extended into virtually every sphere of life. Through countless legal and political battles, African Americans increased the black franchise, gained the right to acquire an equal education, to own property, to enjoy the protection of the law, and to participate in state and federal government—in essence, to enjoy the rights and privileges once reserved for white Americans only. Perhaps most importantly, the civil rights movement laid bare forever the overwhelming barriers—many of which continue to plague minorities today—to full equality.

Because the civil rights movement lost momentum in the aftermath of Martin Luther King's assassination, many scholars mark King's passing in 1968 as the end of the movement. Yet this watershed moment in history continues to be the subject of intense scrutiny as scholars and historians attempt to answer questions and challenge assumptions about the movement. For example, many scholars and observers consider the civil rights movement as part of an ongoing struggle that had begun decades earlier—since emancipated slaves sought to exercise the civil rights promised to them at the end of the Civil War. What, then, catalyzed the modern civil rights movement and why did it gather strength in the 1950s and decline in the 1960s? Why did it become more radical in its later years? How did the movement's leaders and participants—many with diverse strategies, tactics, and goals—effect change?

In the ongoing debate concerning the origins, impact, and legacy of the civil rights movement, many scholars have come to understand the black struggle primarily as a political movement encompassing the national organizations and federal officials that wrought change through judicial and legislative efforts. Others feel that this focal point is too narrow, charging that a comprehensive understanding of the movement must center on the local communities and grassroots individuals and organizations that constituted the backbone of the movement. The following selections address these two viewpoints as they examine the role of national leaders versus local initiatives. They represent, in small part, the large body of contemporary scholarship that continues to explore new dimensions of the civil rights movement.

Viewpoint 1

"Given existing power relationships heavily favoring whites, southern Blacks could not possibly eliminate racial inequality without outside federal assistance."

National Leaders Played the Most Important Role in the Civil Rights Movement

Steven F. Lawson

As contemporary historians debate the many facets of the American civil rights movement—its origins and legacy, for example—one line of scholarship has centered on the role of presidents, lawmakers, and other national leaders in the creation of a more equitable society. Among the leading scholars of civil rights history is Steven F. Lawson, professor of history at Rutgers University. In Lawson's view, the federal government—in tandem with national organizations and leaders—played a crucial role in the civil rights movement through the creation of decisive civil

Steven F. Lawson, "The View from the Nation," *Debating the Civil Rights Movement, 1945–1968*, Steven F. Lawson and Charles Payne. Lanham, MD: Rowman & Littlefield, 1998. Copyright © 1998 by Rowman & Littlefield Publishers, Inc. All rights reserved. Reproduced by permission.

rights legislation and the defeat of state governments that imposed upon blacks a second-class status. In contrast, grassroots movements, despite noble efforts, simply could not have overturned the insidious system of white supremacy without the backing of national organizations and the federal government. According to this "top-down" interpretation, as Lawson calls it, large-scale events, such as the passage of civil rights acts, for example, constitute the most substantive gains of the civil rights revolution. Lawson is the author of several books on the civil rights movement, including *Debating the Civil Rights Movement, 1945–1968*, from which the following viewpoint is excerpted.

It is impossible to understand how Blacks achieved first-class citizenship rights in the South without concentrating on what national leaders in Washington, D.C., did to influence the course of events leading to the extension of racial equality. Powerful presidents, congressional lawmakers, and members of the Supreme Court provided the legal instruments to challenge racial segregation and disfranchisement. Without their crucial support, the struggle against white supremacy in the South still would have taken place but would have lacked the power and authority to defeat state governments intent on keeping Blacks in subservient positions.

Along with national officials, the fate of the civil rights movement depended on the presence of national organizations. Groups such as the National Association for the Advancement of Colored People (NAACP), founded in 1909, drew on financial resources and legal talent from all over the country to press the case for equal rights in Congress and the courts. In similar fashion, Dr. Martin Luther King, Jr., and the Southern Christian Leadership Conference (SCLC), established in the mid-1950s, focused their attention on spotlighting white southern racism before a national audience to mobilize support for their side. Even if white Americans outside the South had wanted to ignore the plight of southern Blacks, NAACP lawyers and lobbyists, SCLC protesters, and their like-minded allies made that choice impossible. They could do what Black residents of local communities could not do alone: turn the civil rights struggle into a national cause for concern and prod the federal government into throwing its considerable power to overturn the entrenched system of white domination that had prevailed for centuries in the South.

Historical accounts that center on the national state in Washington and the operations of national organizations take on a particular narrative. The story begins with World War II, which stimulated Black protests against racism, and winds its way through the presidencies of Franklin D. Roosevelt, Harry S. Truman, Dwight D. Eisenhower, John F. Kennedy, and Lyndon B. Johnson. This period witnessed significant presidential executive orders promulgating desegregation in the military and in housing, five pieces of pioneering civil rights legislation, and landmark Supreme Court rulings toppling segregationist practices and extending the right to vote. The familiar geographical signposts of civil rights demonstrations—Montgomery, Birmingham, Selma, Albany, Little Rock—derive their greatest importance as places that molded the critical national debate on ending racial discrimination.

Overall, a nuanced account of the Black freedom struggle requires an interconnected approach. A balanced portrayal acknowledges that Black activists had important internal resources at their disposal, derived from religious, economic, educational, and civic institutions, with which to make their demands. But it does not belittle African-American creativity and determination to conclude that given existing power relationships heavily favoring whites, southern Blacks could not possibly eliminate racial inequality without outside federal assistance. Furthermore, Washington officials had to protect African Americans from intimidation and violence to allow them to carry out their challenges to discrimination. Without this room for maneuvering, civil rights advocates would encounter insurmountable hurdles in confronting white power.

At the same time, the federal government could shape the direction of the struggle by choosing whether and when to respond to Black protest and by deciding on whom to bestow its support within Black communities. Although united around the struggle against white supremacy, African Americans were not monolithic in their outlook and held various shades of opinion on how best to combat racial bias. By allocating precious resources and conferring recognition on particular elements within local Black communities, national leaders could accelerate or slow down the pace of racial change. . . .

The Supreme Court and School Desegregation

[In 1950], the National Association struck at Jim Crow in higher education. Its chief counsel, Thurgood Marshall, argued that by setting up dual law schools at the University of Texas and segregated graduate facilities at the University of Oklahoma, these state institutions, like those elsewhere in the South, had created separate but not equal opportunities for African Americans. In *Sweatt v. Painter* and *McLaurin v. Board of Regents*, the high tribunal agreed and suggested that increased financial resources to upgrade Black schools could not produce genuine equality, that Black students would have to receive the chance to learn in an environment that did not treat them as inferior. These decisions did not overturn segregation squarely, but they did set the stage for the NAACP to challenge the doctrine of separate but equal head-on in the field of public school education, which would affect white and Black southerners more profoundly than any other challenge thus far.

The assault on public school segregation highlights the crucial role played by the federal government in pushing forward the struggle for civil rights. Initiated by the NAACP and supported by its local branches, the litigation to desegregate the schools culminated in *Brown v. Board of Education*, a series of five cases from (Topeka) Kansas, South Carolina, Virginia, Delaware, and Washington, D.C. In 1954, the Supreme Court put to rest the legal fiction that under a system of enforced racial separation Black students could receive an equal education. Speaking for the high tribunal, Chief Justice Earl Warren did not attack white supremacy directly or castigate southerners for historically oppressing African Americans. Rather, he argued that it was impossible for Blacks to obtain the full benefits of an education under the system of segregation. "We conclude," he asserted, "that in the field of public education the doctrine of 'separate but equal' has no place. Separate educational facilities are inherently unequal."

Although this case pertained solely to public schools, the unanimous Supreme Court justices infused the overall fight for civil rights with constitutional legitimacy. They raised doubts about the validity of segregation as a means of preserving white supremacy. Jim Crow did not automatically crumble, and many obstacles remained; however, the highest federal court in the land had raised a powerful voice on behalf of racial equality and given Blacks hope that the national government was on their side. . . .

The Montgomery Bus Boycott

In Montgomery, Alabama, the "Cradle of the Confederacy," a number of Black groups were promoting voter registration and planning challenges to discriminatory service on city buses. On December 1, 1955, Rosa Parks, a middle-aged Black seamstress, refused to vacate her seat for a white passenger who boarded the bus on which she was riding home after a long day's work. The arrest of this mild-mannered woman sparked a one-year boycott of the buses. A network of local organizations made this protest possible. Parks was an official of the Montgomery chapter of the NAACP, and the president of her branch, E.D. Nixon, arranged for her release from jail and called for a demonstration. The Women's Political Council, led by Jo Ann Gibson Robinson, a college professor, then plotted strategy for a one-day boycott and distributed thousands of flyers to alert people to the plan. They recruited clergy to lend their churches for mass meetings and encourage their congregants to withhold patronage from the buses. They also tapped a relatively new minister in town, the twenty-six-year-old Reverend Martin Luther King, Jr., to head the Montgomery Improvement Association, the coalition established to coordinate the protest.

The year-long campaign showed the growing power of a grassroots movement, but it also proved that the struggle for civil rights desperately needed the federal government to crack determined white southern opposition. By mid-1956, the city still refused to capitulate to Black demands despite the severe economic losses inflicted by the boycott and defections by some white women who drove their maids to work. Coinciding with the boycott, the NAACP had initiated a lawsuit challenging the validity of government-sanctioned bus segregation. In June, the federal district court ruled for the Black plaintiffs; in November, the Supreme Court affirmed the decision. Only after the high tribunal spoke did Montgomery finally abandon segregation on its bus lines. The boycott played a necessary part in pointing the way toward freedom, but without the legal backing of the federal government, it proved an insufficient means of ending Jim Crow. . . .

Little Rock

In 1957, the NAACP had won a federal court decree to desegregate Central High School in the Arkansas capital. Led by Daisy Bates, the association's local president, nine Black youths set out in September to attend school with whites for the first time in their lives. They found their way blocked by Governor Orval Faubus, who posted the national guard around campus to keep the Black students from entering the school. When Eisenhower met with the governor and warned him not to defy the federal court order, Faubus pulled the troops. By this time, however, the governor had inflamed racial passions beyond the boiling point; and when the Little Rock Nine [the first black students to attend Central] attempted to enter the high school, they were turned back by raging mobs.

Faced with this obvious challenge to the federal government, Eisenhower had little choice but to respond with force. The former five-star general dispatched the 101st Airborne Division to Little Rock to preserve the peace and assure the safety of Black students seeking to enter Central. In this episode Eisenhower revealed the enormous might of the federal government while also exposing the reluctance of presidents to deploy it. Concerned about overstepping the boundaries imposed by the Constitution's division of powers between national and state governments, the chief executive had allowed Arkansas as much leeway as possible and intervened only when Washington's authority came under direct attack. Whatever reluctance to use force Eisenhower had shown, his resolution of the crisis had inspired optimism among African Americans. Roger Wilkins, a civil rights activist and scholar who was twenty-five years old at the time, recalled, "Little Rock was a major milestone. We felt the country was becoming more just and the federal government was on our side."

Nevertheless, this incident showed that the national government remained a tentative ally for African Americans. Whatever rights the Constitution guaranteed and the courts affirmed, the federal government was likely to act only if pressured to do so. Events such as Little Rock thus shaped an understandable crisis mentality among civil rights proponents. Appeals to moral conscience went only so far in persuading white officials to combat Jim Crow. Presidents and members of Congress responded to grievances more effectively when Blacks and their white allies exerted substantial political pressure or when their attempts to obtain equality provoked violence from white resisters. In other words, national lawmakers were more likely to respond to the threat of possible racial firestorms than to abstract appeals to justice. In this way, the government helped shape the logic for protest by signaling to Blacks the need to confront racism head-on before Washington would choose to intervene.

Martin Luther King Jr.

Martin Luther King, Jr., was slowly making his way to this conclusion during the 1950s. Following the Montgomery bus boycott, King had created the Southern Christian Leadership Conference in 1957. Consisting mainly of Black ministers, the organization operated as "the political arm of the Black church" and reflected King's commitment to nonviolent direct action as a technique to battle all forms of racism. Not only did the Reverend King seek to convert the hearts and minds of white racists through appeals to their Christian consciences, but he and his followers recognized the necessity of applying political pressure to change racist behavior and practices. Accordingly, Black communities would have to mount sustained mass demonstrations to confront Jim Crow directly, bring the evil of racism out in the open, and goad reforms from white authorities.

In the years after Montgomery, King's efforts came up short. By 1960, massive resistance in the South had kept Black enfranchisement to a minimum and blocked desegregation of public schools and other facilities almost entirely. The federal government had provided some relief through passage of two civil rights acts, but Washington officials preferred that Black citizens voluntarily work out settlements with southern politicians. In taking this approach, national leaders helped to structure the civil rights struggle by forcing Black southerners to devise creative tactics to confront white supremacy. . . .

Birmingham

The federal government refused to flex its considerable muscle on a day-to-day basis in the South, but it did respond to extraordinary circumstances. Eisenhower had shown in Little Rock that the national government would intervene to uphold federal authority when it was directly threatened by state resistance. Kennedy followed suit. He preferred to rely on reasonable dialogue with state officials to persuade them to obey the law, but when such conversations proved futile he had no choice but to act forcefully. Such was the case with the University of Mississippi. The federal courts had ordered the state to admit James Meredith as the first Black student at Ole Miss. Governor Ross Barnett, as had Orval Faubus in Arkansas, strung the president along to delay admission. In October 1962, the governor's stalling tactics heightened white resistance, and when Meredith showed up to attend classes a riot erupted on campus. Only then did the president finally run out of patience and send in federal troops to protect Meredith and quell the disturbance, but not before two people died and 375 were injured. Once again, civil rights proponents learned the hard way that if they wanted federal intervention, they would have to produce a crisis that resulted in the breakdown of public order.

By the spring of 1963 Martin Luther King, Jr., had fully reached this conclusion. One of his aides explained: "To take a moderate approach hoping to get white help, doesn't help. They nail you to the cross, and it saps the enthusiasm of the followers. You've got to have a crisis." He selected Birmingham, Alabama, to provoke federal intervention. The city had a long history of repression of civil rights activists and labor union organizers, and its police commissioner, Eugene "Bull" Connor, used an iron fist to turn back any signs of insurgency. In addition, the Ku Klux Klan and other terrorists had planted bombs to quiet local civil rights proponents such as the Reverend Fred Shuttlesworth, albeit unsuccessfully. Into this cauldron of racial hostility, King brought his troops to stir up the local Black community in a campaign against Jim Crow. Indeed, under Shuttlesworth's fearless direction Birmingham Blacks had already been carrying on protests against segregation, but they had failed to capture the kind of national attention that would force the federal government to render sufficient support.

The protests King spearheaded in April and May sparked federal interest. Unlike King's previous experience in Albany, television cameras and newspaper photographs produced powerful images of peaceful demonstrators suffering brutality at the hands of Bull Connor's law enforcement agents. Snarling police dogs bit demonstrators, and firefighters unleashed high-power water hoses to disperse protesters. Birmingham's jails filled with Black marchers, among them King. When the number of adults available for protest dwindled, King recruited children, some as young as six years old, whose tender age did not keep them from getting assaulted and arrested. Faced with a racial crisis spiraling out of control, the Kennedy administration stepped up its efforts to restore peace. In early May, Justice Department negotiators helped hammer out a settlement that initiated desegregation of restaurants and increased employment opportunities for Blacks. Unfortunately, this agreement did not stop random acts of violence. A few days after the settlement, a bomb exploded at the hotel at which King was staying. Although nobody was hurt, angry Blacks lost patience and pelted police with rocks and bottles. Even more horrible, several months later in September, a more lethal bomb ripped through the basement of a Birmingham church and killed four young Black girls.

The 1964 Civil Rights Act

Birmingham and scores of other demonstrations throughout the South finally prompted President Kennedy to take a strong stand against segregation and exert leadership on behalf of the Black freedom movement. In early June 1963, he sent federal marshals to ensure that Black students gain entry to the University of Alabama. In a stage-managed and highly publicized affair, Governor George Wallace appeared on campus, voiced his objections in front of the administration building, and then stepped aside in

the face of superior federal might. But Kennedy's greatest performance came in a nationally televised address to the American
people. On the evening of June 11, he spoke powerfully about the
ethical imperative of providing African Americans with first-class
citizenship. Civil rights was "a moral issue," he proclaimed, "as
old as the Scriptures and . . . as clear as the Constitution." Deeply
concerned that the "fires of frustration and discord are burning
in every city," the president warned that burgeoning racial crises
"cannot be met by repressive police action" or "quieted by token
moves or talk." These words took on even greater urgency a few
hours later in Jackson, Mississippi, where the NAACP leader
Medgar Evers was gunned down and killed by a sniper.

Kennedy followed up his inspiring address by introducing a
comprehensive civil rights bill in Congress. It aimed mainly at fa-
cilitating school desegregation and opening up public accommodations, such as restaurants and hotels, on an equal basis to Black
customers. Fueled by moral outrage, the measure was nonetheless tempered by political caution. The administration refused to
press for a provision that would create a commission to guarantee equal employment opportunities for minorities, calculating
instead that it would make passage of the bill even more difficult
against southern congressional opposition. However, this did not
stop civil rights supporters in the legislature from adding this proposal to the bill.

The civil rights forces sought to keep the fires of Kennedy's
moral fervor lit by raising the political pressure. A. Philip Randolph now led the massive march on Washington he had first proposed on the eve of World War II. With the NAACP, SCLC,
SNCC, and CORE among others behind him, Randolph called on
Blacks and whites to rally at the nation's capital for jobs and freedom and, more immediately, to express support for the administration's pending civil rights bill. At first, Kennedy urged Black
leaders not to hold the march for fear of creating "an atmosphere
of intimidation" that would scare off uncommitted lawmakers
whose votes were needed to pass the bill. King brushed these objections aside by reminding the president that a well-disciplined,
nonviolent rally would mobilize "support in parts of the country
which don't know the problems first hand." Convinced by the

planners of their peaceful intentions and willingness to refrain from disrupting government business, Kennedy swung his approval behind the march.

The August 28 rally attracted nearly a quarter of a million people and a good deal of favorable publicity. In a dignified manner it spotlighted the interracial vision of brotherhood that had characterized the early years of the civil rights struggle and found voice in the stirring words of King, who recited his dream that "all God's children, black men and white men, Jews and Gentiles, Protestants and Catholics, will be able to join hands and sing in the words of that old Negro spiritual, 'Free at last! Free at last! Thank God almighty, we are free at last.'"

Once again, rhetoric alone, no matter how well meaning, proved insufficient to secure passage of civil rights legislation. The bill was still stalled in the House of Representatives when Kennedy was assassinated on November 22, 1963. A nation's grief could not immediately break the legislative logjam, even as a memorial to the slain president. It took some eight months of painstaking efforts in Congress before a bipartisan coalition of Democrats and Republicans finally overcame southern opposition. On July 2, 1964, the most far-reaching civil rights statute since Reconstruction went into effect. It expanded authority of the federal government to challenge school segregation as well as discrimination in public accommodations and employment. To enforce its provisions, the act set up the Equal Employment Opportunity Commission, established the Community Relations Service, and empowered Washington to cut off federal funds to state and local agencies that practiced racial bias.

Though there were pockets of resistance to it, within a relatively short time Jim Crow signs and barriers were removed from public facilities in the South. Progress in desegregating public schools continued slowly, though the law empowered the federal government to cut off funds from school districts that defied court orders to open their doors to Black students. It would take another four years for the Supreme Court to announce once and for all, in *Green v. County School Board* (1968), that further delay was not constitutionally permissible.

The movement's legislative agenda received a big boost when

Lyndon Baines Johnson entered the White House upon Kennedy's death. The Texan had undergone a stunning transformation with respect to civil rights, from a congressman who had opposed the Truman administration's civil rights program to a vice president who embraced the civil rights movement as a moral and political necessity. Not only was support for racial equality the right thing to do in principle, but it also helped advance Johnson's ambitions to rise to the presidency, recruit enfranchised southern Black voters to the Democratic Party, and give his native South an opportunity to put the corrosive racial issue behind it. Consequently, President Johnson displayed a passion for civil rights advancement that exceeded Kennedy's. A legislative wizard in his days in Congress, Johnson played a large part in engineering passage of the landmark 1964 law. . . .

By the end of the 1960s the civil rights movement, as it had existed for over two decades, had come to a conclusion. Martin Luther King fell to an assassin's bullet in April 1968, and though the SCLC remained in operation, it never recovered from the loss of its charismatic head. With SNCC and CORE on the decline, this left the NAACP and the National Urban League (NUL), as the major survivors of the old civil rights alliance. The moderates had scored three major legislative victories and won numerous battles in the courts to enforce desegregation and disfranchisement. However, even moderation was not enough to sustain the struggle at the national level once conservatives captured the White House beginning with Richard Nixon in 1968. For the most part, the civil rights groups that remained in existence sought to preserve thc legislative and judicial victories they had obtained and see that they were properly enforced.

Viewpoint 2

"The real accomplishments of the black freedom struggle stemmed . . . from the efforts of the grass roots organizers who actually built and directed the movement in the South."

Grassroots Organizers Played the Most Important Role in the Civil Rights Movement

David J. Garrow

David J. Garrow is a presidential distinguished professor at Emory University Law School. He is the author of numerous books and articles about the civil rights movement, including *Bearing the Cross: Martin Luther King, Jr., and the Southern Christian Leadership Conference.* In the following viewpoint, Garrow challenges civil rights scholarship that focuses primarily on the policies and actions of nationally oriented—and commonly identified—civil rights organizations and leaders. To

Garrow, the real backbone of the movement was a cadre of crucial—albeit lesser known—grassroots leaders. As testament, Garrow offers several examples of unsung heroes—ordinary people who directed and sustained the movement and exerted a great personal impact on national events. Grassroots workers Diane Nash and James Bevel, for example, engaged in activities that were, in fact, catalytic to the passage of the 1965 Voting Rights Acts. The following viewpoint is excerpted from *The Civil Rights Movement in America*, an anthology of perspectives on civil rights history.

Too often those who write about the civil rights movement employ too narrow and exclusive a concept of "leadership." Implicitly if not explicitly, they presume that leaders are simply those individuals who are organizational chieftains or spokespersons. They thus restrict our definition of leadership to administrators and articulators, without looking as carefully and as thoughtfully as they should for a more meaningful understanding of "leadership."

This overly narrow conception of leadership runs directly parallel to a similar tendency to devote a disproportionate amount of scholarly attention to the national civil rights organizations of the 1950s and 1960s—the National Association for the Advancement of Colored People (NAACP), the Southern Christian Leadership Conference (SCLC), the Student Nonviolent Coordinating Committee (SNCC), the National Urban League (NUL) and the Congress of Racial Equality (CORE). While concentrating studies on those organizations and the individuals who headed them—Roy Wilkins, Martin Luther King, Jr., John Lewis and Stokely Carmichael, Whitney Young, and James Farmer—simultaneously far too little scholarly attention has been devoted to local level civil rights activities and to the grass roots organizers who actually mobilized people to participate actively in the movement.

In the 1950s, the major strategic difference of opinion that existed among black civil rights activists was a division between those who believed that courtroom litigation and judicial decisions were the principal means for advancing black freedom and those who contended that ordinary, grass roots people could take a direct and meaningful hand in pursuing their own freedom. While NAACP Executive Secretary Roy Wilkins and NAACP Legal Defense and Educational Fund director Thurgood Marshall argued that the lawyerly expansion of the principles articulated by the Supreme Court in *Brown v. Board of Education of Topeka* was the surest route to further black gains, Brotherhood of Sleeping Car Porters president A. Philip Randolph and others colleagues maintained that mass action, and not simply elite-sponsored litigation, could bring about substantial racial change.

Those mass action proponents welcomed the Montgomery, Alabama, bus boycott of 1955–1956 as precisely the sort of opening round in a new, mass-based southern freedom struggle they long had hoped for. Similarly, those activists also welcomed the 1957 formation of the ministerially-oriented SCLC and the largely spontaneous black college student sit-in movement that spread like wildfire across the South during the spring and early summer of 1960. On the other hand, NAACP administrators contended that it was only a federal court ruling, not the mass boycott, that actually desegregrated Montgomery's buses, and they regretted both the formation of SCLC and the appearance of SNCC, which grew out of the 1960 sit-ins. Within just a few years' time, both SCLC and SNCC, employing different tactical choices, made the mass action strategy the dominant approach of the 1960s black freedom struggle.

That deeply-rooted strategic division in central both to the subsequent history of inter-organizational relations within the movement and to the malapportionment of scholarly attention over the past two decades. Like the one-time chieftains of the elite-oriented civil rights organizations, many scholars have presumed that the policies, statements and actions of the national civil rights organizations are the most importance substance of the movement's history. However, a more discerning look at the movement's actual record of achievement in the south, and in the national political arena, reveals, upon careful examination, that the real accomplishments of the black freedom struggle stemmed not so much from the activities of the administrators and articulators as from the efforts of the grass roots organizers who actually built and directed the movement in the South.

Influential Leaders

To say that most of the work of the movement was not done by the commonly-identified leaders would seem obvious to all. The basic point, however, in considerably broader than that: what the carefully-scrutinized historical record shows is that the actual human catalysts of the movement, the people who really gave direction to the movement's organizing work, the individuals whose records reflect the greatest substantive accomplishments, were not administrators or spokespersons, and were not those whom most scholarship on the movement identifies as the "leaders." Instead, in any list, long or short, of the activists who had the greatest personal impact upon the course of the southern movement, the vast majority of names will be ones that are unfamiliar to most readers. Allow six brief examples to suffice. In Mississippi, no other individuals did more to give both political direction and emotional sustenance to movement activists than Robert Parris Moses, a SNCC field worker who became the guiding force in COFO, the Council of Federated Organizations, and Fannie Lou Hamer, the relatively unlettered but impressively articulate Sunflower County tenant farmer's wife who in 1964 emerged as an influential grass roots spokeswoman for the thousands of economically poor black citizens who actually comprised the movement's base.

In southwest Georgia, another major scene of movement activism, the guiding spirit of much of the effort there, from the time of his initial arrival in Terrell County as the sole paid field secretary of SNCC to [1990], when he served on the Albany city council, was Charles Sherrod, a little-heralded organizer who deserves much of the credit for sparking and sustaining the entire southwest Georgia movement. Although Sherrod, like Moses, was an "outside agitator" initially sent in by SNCC, in Selma, Alabama, one of the movement's famous battlegrounds, the key individual figure was a longtime native, Mrs. Amelia P. Boynton, whose impact there was much like Mrs. Hamer's in Mississippi. A crucial figure in organizing the initial indigenous activism, in first bringing SNCC workers to Selma, and in persuading Dr. King and SCLC to make Selma the focal point of their 1965 voting rights protests, Mrs. Boynton had as substantial an impact on civil rights developments in Alabama as anyone, excepting perhaps only Birmingham's Reverend

Fred L. Shuttlesworth, another widely-underestimated and under-appreciated grass roots leader.

Diane Nash and James Bevel

Lastly, inside of SNCC and SCLC, two individuals who had crucial but often-overlooked roles in repeatedly influencing important movement decisions were Diane Nash and James Bevel, both of whom emerged from the Nashville movement of 1959–1961. Nash played a central part in sustaining the 1961 Freedom Rides when white Alabama violence threatened to halt them, and her April, 1962 memo reprimanding movement activists for not always living up in practice to their much-touted slogan of "jail, no bail" had a significant impact on King and dozens of others. Together with Bevel, Nash in September, 1963, originated one of the most important strategic gameplans of the southern struggle. Four months earlier Bevel, a young SCLC staff aide, had been personally responsible for SCLC's crucial tactical decision to send young children into the streets of Birmingham during the height of the protests there, the crucial turning point in convincing white business leaders to grant the movement's demands and an important influence on President John F. Kennedy's decision to send to Congress the bill that eventually became the 1964 Civil Rights Act. Nash and Bevel, in the immediate aftermath of the Birmingham church bombing that killed four young girls, envisioned a comprehensive mass action campaign to close down the regular functioning of Alabama state of government and "GROW"—Get Rid Of [Alabama governor George C.] Wallace. Though rejected by King, and other organization heads at that time, the Nash/Bevel blueprint started King and SCLC on an Alabama Project that eighteen months later, following various changes and refinements, culminated in the landmark Selma-to-Montgomery march and congressional passage of the 1965 Voting Rights Act.

Backbone of the Movement

It takes nothing away from King, Wilkins, Whitney Young or James Farmer to acknowledge that Moses, Hamer, Sherrod, Boynton, Nash and Bevel equally merit the designation as civil rights "leaders" if that label is to be applied in its most substantively meaningful way. Indeed, it could be argued further, with considerable justification, that catalytic grass root workers like those six deserve the appellation more than do New York-based bureaucrats such as Wilkins and Young. The real emergence of a sustained and widespread movement in the South can be traced, in many particulars, to the August, 1961, SNCC decision to create a cadre of locally-based, full time grass roots organizers, the first time that indigenous activists in many areas of the rural Deep South had such day-to-day organizational assistance available to them. Those full-time workers, usually affiliated with SNCC, CORE or SCLC, constituted the real backbone of the southern movement during the years of its greatest activism and achievements, 1961–1966. Similarly, the somewhat precipitous decline of the southern freedom struggle between 1966 and 1968 can also largely be traced to the burnout and eventual departure from full time organizing of most of that crucial cadre. Although this is not the place to make the argument in its most extended form, it was the interaction between the existing indigenous activists and these full time field secretaries that generated most of the actual "leadership" of the southern struggle. As many SNCC veterans in particular can well articulate, it was the first-hand experience of working with people, day in, day out, that educated both local activists and field secretaries to the item-by-item, conversation-by-conversation reality of what "leadership" really amounted to in the civil rights movement.

The best of the national organization chieftains and spokespersons, namely King, Lewis and Farmer, all privately appreciated how their heavy responsibilities for making speeches, raising funds, and stimulating organizational publicity oftentimes excessively drew them away from the real, hands on work of the movement. King and Farmer in particular were troubled by how their administrative tasks and the "organization maintenance" needs of SCLC and CORE often took priority over any opportunities for sustained personal involvement in the activities that constituted the real purpose of their organizations. Thus at least these men, if not all of the other administrators and articulators of movement organizations, realized full well that leadership of the freedom struggle lay in many, many hands other than those of the "Big, Six" organization heads often singled out by the news media.

For Further Discussion

Chapter 1

1. Compare the policies of W.E.B. Du Bois and Booker T. Washington. Whose program promised more immediate gains for blacks? Was it possible for blacks to better their condition without pressing for the political and social rights advocated by Du Bois?

2. Was Washington's case for black accommodation to white society an appropriate response to black grievances when viewed in a historical context? Why did Washington's policies fall out of popularity after his death in 1915?

3. Even before the heyday of the civil rights movement in the mid–twentieth century, the black freedom struggle was characterized by both judicial activism and social activism. Did the legal machinery of the National Association for the Advancement of Colored People (NAACP) preclude or insubstantiate A. Philip Randolph's ideas on mass-action campaigns, or did the two approaches complement one another?

Chapter 2

1. What evidence does Thurgood Marshall give to counter James Jackson Kilpatrick's claim that southern racial practices were relatively benign?

2. Why did the authors and signers of the Southern Manifesto find the Supreme Court's decision in *Brown v. Board of Education* an abuse of judicial power? Explain how both Earl Warren and the Southern Manifesto authors use *Plessy v. Ferguson* to bolster their antithetical views regarding school segregation.

3. Does Louis Anthes successfully back up his argument that the *Brown v. Board of Education* verdict was ultimately self-defeating in its portrayal of blacks as powerless victims? Given his views, how might Julius L. Chambers answer Anthes's criticism of *Brown*?

Chapter 3

1. To what extent is John F. Kennedy's call for federal civil rights legislation an emotional appeal to Americans? Similarly, how does James Farmer present his claim that federal and state efforts are inadequate?
2. Describe Martin Luther King Jr.'s program of nonviolence as a strategy for advancing civil rights. At the same time, compare King's views to those of Malcolm X. Why did the latter feel that it was impossible to keep the movement for civil rights nonviolent?
3. How does Stokely Carmichael justify the rise of black-power politics in the 1960s? What were the advantages and disadvantages of this increasingly militant outlook? Does Kenneth Clark's criticism of this trend seem justified?
4. Did the mass-action campaigns led by King successfully publicize black demands? Did they pave the way for the legal victories of the NAACP?

Chapter 4

1. Steven F. Lawson cites *Brown v. Board of Education* as a testament to the tremendous power wielded by the federal government. In your view, did the Supreme Court ruling pertaining to school desegregation extend beyond the public schools to accelerate the pace of civil rights in general? If so, does this lend credibility to Lawson's analysis of the role of the federal government?
2. What evidence does David J. Garrow give to support his contention that grassroots activists exerted enormous influence over national events? In your opinion, was grassroots activity critical to the success of the civil rights movement?

❋ Chronology

1895

Booker T. Washington delivers his Atlanta Exposition speech, which accepts segregation of the races.

1896

The Supreme Court rules in *Plessy v. Ferguson* that separate but equal treatment of the races is constitutional.

1905

The Niagara Movement is founded by W.E.B. Du Bois and other black leaders to urge more direct action to achieve black civil rights.

1909

The National Association for the Advancement of Colored People (NAACP) is organized.

1910

National Urban League is founded to help the conditions of urban African Americans.

1931

Farrad Muhammad establishes in Detroit what will become the Black Muslim Movement.

1941

A. Philip Randolph threatens a massive march on Washington unless the Roosevelt administration takes measures to ensure black employment in defense industries; Roosevelt agrees to establish Fair Employment Practices Committee (FEPC).

1942

The Congress of Racial Equality (CORE) is organized in Chicago.

1943

Race riots in Detroit and Harlem cause black leaders to ask their followers to be less demanding in asserting their commitment to civil rights; A. Philip Randolph breaks ranks to call for civil disobedience against Jim Crow schools and railroads.

1946

The Supreme Court, in *Morgan v. The Commonwealth of Virginia*, rules that state laws requiring racial segregation on buses violates the Constitution when applied to interstate passengers.

April 9–23, 1947

Bayard Rustin organizes integrated group trips on trains and buses through Kentucky, Tennessee, North Carolina, and Virginia.

October 29, 1947

To Secure These Rights, the report by the President's Committee on Civil Rights, is released; the commission appointed by President Harry S. Truman calls for the elimination of racial segregation and recommends government action to secure civil rights for all Americans.

July 26, 1948

President Harry S. Truman issues an executive order desegregating the armed services.

May 17, 1954

In *Brown v. Board of Education* the Supreme Court declares separate educational facilities "inherently unequal."

May 31, 1955

Supreme Court, rejecting the NAACP's plea for complete and total desegregation by September 1955, orders desegregation "with all deliberate speed."

September 23, 1955

An all-white jury finds defendants innocent of murdering black teenager Emmett Till after nationally publicized trial; the defendants later confess to the killing.

November 1955

The Interstate Commerce Commission (ICC) bans racial segregation in all facilities and vehicles engaged in interstate transportation.

December 1, 1955
Rosa Parks is arrested for refusing to give up her bus seat to a white person; the action triggers a bus boycott in Montgomery, Alabama, led by Martin Luther King Jr.

February 3, 1956
Autherine Lucy wins a federal court order admitting her to the University of Alabama only to have the university permanently "expel" her; the University of Alabama remains segregated for seven more years.

December 21, 1956
The Montgomery bus boycott ends after city receives U.S. Supreme Court order to desegregate city buses.

January 11, 1957
Martin Luther King Jr. and a number of southern black clergymen create the Southern Christian Leadership Conference (SCLC).

August 29, 1957
Congress passes the first civil rights legislation since Reconstruction: The Civil Rights Act of 1957 establishes a civil rights division at the Justice Department and provides penalties for violating the voting rights of a U.S. citizen.

September 4, 1957
On the orders of Arkansas governor Orval Faubus, Arkansas National Guardsmen block nine black students from entering Central High School in Little Rock.

September 24, 1957
President Dwight D. Eisenhower dispatches one thousand paratroopers of the 101st Airborne Division to Little Rock to enforce a federal court order integrating Central High School.

September 29, 1958
The Supreme Court, in *Cooper v. Aaron*, rules that "evasive schemes" cannot be used to circumvent school desegregation.

1959

Sit-in campaigns by college students desegregate eating facilities in St. Louis, Chicago, and Bloomington, Indiana; the Tennessee Christian Leadership Conference holds brief sit-ins in Nashville department stores.

February 1, 1960

Four black students stage a sit-in at a Woolworth's lunch counter in Greensboro, North Carolina; the sit-in movement to desegregate southern restaurants, hotels, movie theaters, libraries, and parks spreads to other southern states.

April 1960

The Student Nonviolent Coordinating Committee (SNCC) is formed at a student conference in Raleigh, North Carolina.

May 6, 1960

President Eisenhower signs civil rights legislation authorizing federal judges to appoint referees to assist blacks seeking to register and to vote.

October 19, 1960

Martin Luther King Jr. is arrested during an Atlanta sit-in; Democratic presidential candidate John F. Kennedy telephones Mrs. King to express concern.

December 5, 1960

The Supreme Court rules that discrimination in bus terminal restaurants is a violation of the Interstate Commerce Act.

March 13, 1961

James Farmer, national director of CORE, calls for volunteers to conduct "Freedom Rides" throughout the South.

May 1961

White and black freedom riders are arrested and assaulted in North and South Carolina and Alabama; one bus is burned by a white mob. The CORE-sponsored Freedom Ride disbands and the movement is taken over by SNCC volunteers; the Kennedy administration sends federal marshals to assure the safety of the freedom riders.

November 1961
Local black organizations in Albany, Georgia, form the Albany Movement to demonstrate for voting rights and desegregation.

December 11–14, 1961
Hundreds of demonstrators participate in marches in Albany, Georgia. Martin Luther King Jr. and aides arrive on December 15.

May 31, 1962
James Meredith files suit claiming racial discrimination after he is denied admission into the University of Mississippi.

August 1962
Albany Movement ends with many of its goals unmet.

August 7, 1962
A SNCC Voter Registration School opens in Pike County, Mississippi, marking the first such effort in the history of the state.

September 30, 1962
President Kennedy federalizes the National Guard and sends several hundred federal marshals to Mississippi to guarantee James Meredith's admission to the University of Mississippi Law School over the opposition of Governor Ross Barnett and other whites; two persons are killed in a campus riot.

November 20, 1962
President Kennedy signs an executive order barring racial discrimination in federally financed housing.

February 2, 1963
Martin Luther King Jr. and other SCLC leaders arrive in Birmingham, Alabama, to lead a civil rights campaign.

Spring 1963
CORE takes the lead in protesting discrimination in northern cities.

April 1963

Martin Luther King Jr. opens his campaign to desegregate Birmingham and is arrested on April 12; while incarcerated King composes his "Letter from Birmingham City Jail."

May 3, 1963

Birmingham police chief Eugene "Bull" Connor turns police dogs and fire hoses against nonviolent demonstrators in Birmingham.

May 5, 1963

Three thousand protesters are jailed in Birmingham—the largest number of people imprisoned at any one time in the history of the civil rights movement.

May 10, 1963

An accord is reached in Birmingham; within ninety days lunch counters, rest rooms, and drinking fountains will be desegregated in the city.

June 11, 1963

Black students Vivian Malone and James Hood enter the University of Alabama despite a demonstration of resistance by Governor George Wallace; in a nationally televised speech President John F. Kennedy calls segregation morally wrong.

June 12, 1963

NAACP field secretary Medgar Evers is shot and killed as he enters his home in Jackson, Mississippi.

August 28, 1963

Over 250,000 Americans gather at the Lincoln Memorial to urge the passage of civil rights legislation and hear Martin Luther King Jr. deliver his "I Have A Dream" speech. Malcolm X dismisses the march as "the Farce on Washington."

September 15, 1963

Four young girls are killed when a bomb explodes at a Baptist church in Birmingham, Alabama.

April 26, 1964

SNCC workers organize the Mississippi Freedom Democratic Party (MFDP).

Summer 1964

Enlisting the help of white volunteers, SNCC and CORE seek to register black voters across the South in the "Freedom Summer" campaign.

June 21, 1964

Three civil rights workers, Michael Schwerner and Andrew Goodman, both white New Yorkers, and James Chaney, a black student from Meridian, Mississippi, are murdered near Philadelphia, Mississippi.

July 2, 1964

President Lyndon Johnson signs the Civil Rights Act of 1964, which prohibits discrimination in most public accommodations, authorizes the federal government to withhold funds from programs practicing discrimination, and creates the Equal Employment Opportunity Commission.

August 22–26, 1964

At the Democratic National Convention in Atlantic City, New Jersey, delegates of the Mississippi Freedom Democratic Party ask to be seated as the legitimate Democratic Party of Mississippi; they refuse the compromise offer of two delegate seats.

December 10, 1964

Martin Luther King Jr. is awarded the Nobel Peace Prize.

February 18, 1965

Civil rights marcher Jimmie Lee Jackson is shot and killed in Marion, Alabama.

February 21, 1965

Malcolm X is assassinated while addressing a rally of his followers in New York City; three black men are ultimately convicted of the murder.

March 7, 1965
"Bloody Sunday": six hundred marchers just outside Selma, Alabama, are attacked by state troopers with nightsticks and tear gas.

March 9, 1965
Martin Luther King Jr. leads a voting rights march in Selma but turns back before a state trooper barricade.

March 11, 1965
The death of white Unitarian minister James J. Reeb following a beating by local whites in Selma triggers demonstrations in many northern cities.

March 21–25, 1965
Following a federal judge's court order allowing the march, and under federalized protection, Martin Luther King Jr. leads a voting rights march from Selma to Montgomery, Alabama.

August 6, 1965
President Johnson signs the Voting Rights Act of 1965, which outlaws literacy tests and empowers the Justice Department to supervise federal elections in seven southern states.

August 11–16, 1965
Rioting in the black ghetto of Watts in Los Angeles leads to thirty-five deaths, nine hundred injuries, and over thirty-five hundred arrests.

January 1966
Martin Luther King Jr. moves to Chicago to begin his first civil rights campaign in a northern city.

March 25, 1966
The Supreme Court bans poll taxes for all elections.

May 16, 1966
Stokely Carmichael replaces John Lewis as chairman of SNCC.

June 6, 1966
James Meredith is shot by a sniper while on a one-man "march against fear" in Mississippi.

June 7–26, 1966
Other civil rights leaders, including King and Carmichael, complete the "Meredith march"; the slogan "black power" is first used by Carmichael.

July 1966
The CORE national convention adopts a resolution in support of black power; the NAACP convention officially opposes the doctrine.

August 5, 1966
Martin Luther King Jr. leads an integrated march in Chicago and is wounded when whites throw bottles and bricks at demonstrators.

October 1966
The Black Panther Party (BPP) is founded in Oakland, California.

December 1966
SNCC votes to exclude whites from membership.

June 13, 1967
Thurgood Marshall is the first black to be nominated to serve on the Supreme Court.

February 25, 1967
Martin Luther King Jr. delivers his first speech devoted entirely to the war in Vietnam, which he calls "one of history's most cruel and senseless wars"; his position causes estrangement with President Johnson and is criticized by the NAACP.

May 10–11, 1967
Rioting at all-black Jackson State College in Mississippi leads to one death and two serious injuries.

June 19, 1967
A federal judge orders Washington, D.C., schools to end de facto school segregation.

July 1967

Rioting in the black ghetto of Newark, New Jersey, leaves 23 dead and 725 injured; Rioting in Detroit leave 43 dead and 324 injured; President Johnson appoints Governor Otto Kerner of Illinois to head a commission to investigate recent urban riots.

February 29, 1968

The Kerner Commission issues its report, warning that the nation is "moving toward two societies, one black, one white—separate and unequal."

March 18, 1968

Martin Luther King Jr. travels to Memphis, Tennessee, to help settle a garbage workers strike.

April 4, 1968

Martin Luther King Jr. is assassinated by James Earl Ray in Memphis, Tennessee, precipitating riots in more than one hundred cities.

April 11, 1968

Congress passes civil rights legislation prohibiting racial discrimination in the sale or rental of housing.

May 11, 1968

Ralph Abernathy, Martin Luther King Jr.'s successor as head of the SCLC, leads Poor People's Campaign in Washington, D.C.

October 30, 1969

The Supreme Court replaces its 1954 decision calling for "all deliberate speed" in school desegregation by unanimously ordering that all segregation in schools must end "at once."

For Further Research

Books

Donzaleigh Abernathy, *Partners to History: Martin Luther King, Jr., Ralph Abernathy, and the Civil Rights Movement.* New York: Crown, 2003.

Ralph Abernathy, *And the Walls Came Tumbling Down.* New York: Harper & Row, 1989.

Jack Bass and Walter De Vries, *Transformation of Southern Politics: Social Change and Political Consequence Since 1945.* New York: BasicBooks, 1976.

Taylor Branch, *Parting the Waters: America in the King Years, 1954–1963.* New York: Simon & Schuster, 1988.

Stewart Burns, *To the Mountaintop: Martin Luther King Jr.'s Sacred Mission to Save America, 1955–1968.* New York: HarperSanFrancisco, 2004.

Devon W. Carbado and Donald Weise, *Time on Two Crosses: The Collected Writings of Bayard Rustin.* San Francisco: Cleis, 2003.

Clayborne Carson, ed., *The Movement: 1964–1970.* New York: Greenwood, 1993.

Bettye Collier-Thomas and V.P. Franklin, eds., *Sisters in the Struggle: African American Women in the Civil Rights–Black Power Movement.* New York: New York University Press, 2004.

James Farmer, *Lay Bare the Heart: An Autobiography of the Civil Rights Movement.* New York: Arbor House, 1985.

Leon Friedman, ed., *The Civil Rights Reader: Basic Documents of the Civil Rights Movement.* New York: Walker, 1968.

Frye Gaillard, *Cradle of Freedom: Alabama and the Movement That Changed America.* Tuscaloosa: University of Alabama Press, 2004.

David J. Garrow, ed., *We Shall Overcome: The Civil Rights Movement in the United States in the 1950s and 1960s.* Brooklyn, NY: Carlson, 1989.

Peter Goldman, *The Death and Life of Malcolm X.* Chicago: University of Chicago Press, 1979.

Paul Goodman, *Of One Blood: Abolitionism and the Origins of Racial Equality.* Berkeley and Los Angeles: University of California Press, 1998.

Grace Elizabeth Hale, *Making Whiteness: The Culture of Segregation in the South, 1890–1940.* New York: Pantheon, 1998.

Martin Luther King Jr., *Where Do We Go from Here? Chaos or Community?* New York: Harper & Row, 1967.

———, *Why We Can't Wait.* New York: Harper & Row, 1963.

Michael J. Klarman, *From Jim Crow to Civil Rights: The Supreme Court and the Struggle for Racial Equality.* New York: Oxford University Press, 2004.

Steven F. Lawson, *Civil Rights Crossroads: Nation, Community, and the Black Freedom Struggle.* Lexington: University Press of Kentucky, 2003.

Peter B. Levy, ed., *Let Freedom Ring: A Documentary History of the Civil Rights Movement.* New York: Praeger, 1992.

Aldon D. Morris, *The Origins of the Civil Rights Movement: Black Communities Organizing for Change.* New York: Free Press, 1984.

Charles Payne, *I've Got the Light of Freedom: The Organizing Tradition and the Mississippi Freedom Struggle.* Berkeley and Los Angeles: University of California Press, 1995.

Charles Payne and Adam Green, eds., *Time Longer than Rope: A Century of African American Activism, 1850–1950.* New York: New York University Press, 2003.

Fred Powledge, *Free at Last? The Civil Rights Movement and the People Who Made It.* Boston: Little, Brown, 1991.

William T. Martin Riches, *The Civil Rights Movement: Struggle and Resistance*. New York: Palgrave Macmillan, 2004.

Bayard Rustin, *Down the Line*. Chicago: Quadrangle, 1971.

Fredrik Sunnemark, *Ring Out Freedom! The Voice of Martin Luther King, Jr., and the Making of the Civil Rights Movement*. Bloomington: Indiana University Press, 2004.

Herman Talmadge, *You and Segregation*. Birmingham, AL: Vulcan, 1955.

James M. Washington, ed., *A Testament of Hope*. San Francisco: Harper & Row, 1986.

Juan Williams, *Eyes on the Prize: America's Civil Rights Years, 1954–1965*. New York: Viking, 1987.

Web Sites

Africanaonline, www.africanaonline.com. This Web site offers extensive information on African American issues, including the civil rights movement and its leaders. Biographical information, primary-source material, and articles are available.

History Net/African American History, http://Afroamhistory.com. This comprehensive site maintains information and links to other sites about the events, leaders, and court cases that impacted the civil rights movement.

King Center, www.thekingcenter.org. The King Center, established in 1968 by Coretta Scott King, offers a wide variety of programs and educational resources, including the King Library and Archives, the world's largest repository of primary-source material on Martin Luther King Jr. and other leaders.

❀ Index